Learning
to Be
YOU

Learning to Be YOU

HOW OUR TRUE IDENTITY IN CHRIST SETS US FREE

David D. Swanson

BakerBooks

a division of Baker Publishing Group
Grand Rapids, Michigan

Published by Baker Books
a division of Baker Publishing Group
P.O. Box 6287, Grand Rapids, MI 49516-6287
www.bakerbooks.com

Printed in the United States of America

Library of Congress Cataloging-in-Publication Data
Swanson, David D., 1963–
    Learning to be you : how our true identity in Christ sets us free / David D. Swanson.
        p. cm.
    ISBN 978-0-8010-1445-1 (pbk.)
    1. Identity (Psychology)—Religious aspects—Christianity. 2. Self-perception—Religious aspects—Christianity. I. Title.
BV4509.5.S925 2012
248.4—dc23   2012006178

The internet addresses, email addresses, and phone numbers in this book are accurate at the time of publication. They are provided as a resource. Baker Publishing Group does not endorse them or vouch for their content or permanence.

Published in association with the literary agency of Wolgemuth & Associates, Inc.

12 13 14 15 16 17 18   7 6 5 4 3 2 1

To my dad, Don Swanson, who taught me what it means to be a man. Gentle. Giving. Faithful. Steadfast. He's the best man I know.

To my spiritual father, Bill Dudley, who taught me how to be a spiritual leader and a pastor, how to laugh in the midst of adversity, and how to serve in the midst of crisis.

Contents

Acknowledgments

As I look back on my life and ministry to this point, it is a sheer act of God's grace that has brought me here. I acknowledge it is only by his faithfulness, his constant provision, his wise and gentle counsel, and his abiding love that I draw breath each day and have the privilege of serving in the life of his church. Writing this book has been beyond my wildest dreams, and yet again God brought people and experiences together as only he can. I am deeply and humbly grateful to God for this and all his many blessings.

When I wrote my first book, *Vital Signs*, I learned that the process of getting a book to completion is a collaborative one that involves a significant number of people. A book is hardly the work of an author alone, and through writing this second book, I am even more aware of that—and grateful for the many who have helped me along the way.

I am grateful to my wife, Leigh, who is always my first editor and my most honest, caring critic. I would be nowhere with this book, or much of anything else, without her. I am also grateful to my children, John David, Alex, and Kaylee.

They fill my life with laughter and joy while always helping me not to take myself too seriously.

I am grateful to Robert and Andrew Wolgemuth for the many hours they have invested in this project and in me. Their unflagging belief in me has been a constant source of encouragement. I am also grateful to the men of the ARK—the faithful brothers I am privileged to share life with each week as we seek to follow Christ. Robb, John, Mike, and Dayne are an invaluable source of wisdom, accountability, and joy.

I am grateful to the pastoral leadership team of First Presbyterian Church, Orlando—a group of men and women who are so gifted and so capable that it frees me to do the things God has called me to do in ministry. What a joy it has been to work with them, to see God's hand, and to share our lives together: Dr. Rebecca Bedell, Minister of Worship; Rev. Sam Knight, Associate for Congregational Life; Rev. Donna McClellan, Associate for Prayer and Spiritual Formation; Dr. Case Thorp, Associate for Mission and Evangelism; and Mr. John Watts, Church Business Administrator.

My two assistants, Paula Lindrum and Grace Whitlow, make my life hum. I cannot imagine how I could function without them in their unique roles: Paula with The Well and Grace at First Presbyterian Church. They are not the least bit impressed with me, and they keep me firmly grounded!

Chad Allen and Baker Books have been a huge help as well. From the beginning, Chad has helped me to be a better writer, and while I am probably not the easiest person in the world to work with, his counsel has been welcome and needed.

Finally, I want to thank the saints of First Presbyterian Church, Orlando, who daily allow me the privilege of being their pastor, of living my life out before them, of tripping and falling and getting back up. They are saints who love me graciously and well.

Introduction

It happened to me again the other day.

I'm on my sofa, mindlessly flipping channels with my remote control, trying to find something edifying to watch on television. I come across a popular talk show and notice a famous actor is the guest. I turn the volume up just in time to hear his long and harrowing journey toward "finding himself." It's a term I hear a lot, inside the church and outside the church. People want to "find themselves." They want to become secure in their identity in the world. For example, when I went to seminary, I was surprised at how many of my fellow students had come in the hope of finding themselves. They were disillusioned with their jobs or experiences, so they left those things behind—even very lucrative careers— hoping that studying theology would somehow unlock the mystery to their true identity. While I appreciate the desire to study theology, such a motive is not the purpose of going to seminary! Others dabble in New Age religious practice or travel to distant lands on pilgrimage or begin new hobbies or rituals like yoga. Regardless, their motivation is the same: they cannot grasp who they are, so they go looking.

My preaching professor in seminary, Dr. Robert Shelton, used to say, "If you're going to be a good preacher, you have to keep the Bible in one hand and a newspaper in the other. You have to be a keen observer of life." I cannot tell you how many times those words have echoed in my head, and I have worked hard to make that my practice.

My observations have led me to conclude that an increasing number of people are on an ill-defined mission to find themselves. By definition, if you have to find yourself, then you are lost. It's a bit like when Mark Twain boarded a train for a trip north. The porters were quite pleased to have such a famous man aboard, but when they came to his car to punch his ticket, he could not find it. Twain started looking furiously, but to no avail. The porter said, "Sir, it's fine. I know who you are. You don't have to find your ticket. Relax and enjoy your trip." Several hours later, the porter came back through the car only to find Twain still looking for his ticket. Again, he tried to reassure him.

"Sir, you really don't have to do that. I know who you are. There is no need for you to find that ticket." With that, Twain stood up and said firmly to the porter, "Listen, young man, I know who I am too. That's not the problem. The problem is I don't know where I'm going!"

At times, we don't know either. We may know our names. We may even know something about our history, but we have no security in where we are or where we are heading. We have become dislocated from ourselves. At least Mark Twain knew his name. I'm assuming most of us at least know that, but we are still on this journey to *find ourselves*—a journey often fraught with missteps and poor choices.

I am continually amazed by the process people use to accomplish this mission. In their quest to find themselves, they are willing to try any and all manner of practice, thought, ideology, and philosophy. They are dining at a buffet of sorts. They try one entrée and then another, all in the hope that one of them will finally satisfy the hunger within. They never find one, so they keep going back, gorging themselves on the false promises of our time. Meditation, Eastern Mysticism, hedonism, kabala, Scientology, objectivism, Buddhism, materialism—the list is endless, and they all become *religions* to people in pursuit of themselves.

Finding yourself is another way of describing this growing spiritual hunger demonstrated in cultures around the world. The more we see external structures in disarray—from the economy, to international terrorism, to natural disasters—the more likely we are to seek answers to the question of ultimate things. We know this life, with all its pain, suffering, hardship, and injustice, cannot be the end. Surely there must be a greater purpose for our existence than the emptiness we see before us.

What's more, the feeling won't leave us alone. It keeps nagging us, making us search for the key that unlocks the mystery. It makes us search and search until we find our way back to our Creator. When we do that, the mystery is unlocked. Here's the deal: you'll never find yourself—you'll never live out of your true identity—until you know the God who made you. Know God, know you. No God, no you. Quite simple, yet largely misunderstood.

Many people are exploring their identity, learning to be who they are, but they are doing so in the absence of God. It's a bit like getting a new car but not getting an owner's manual. The manufacturer knows everything about the vehicle, but we don't have that information. Instead, we blindly try to figure it out by ourselves. Left to that plan, I may wind up putting orange juice in my gas tank because I don't know any better. When that happens, the car quits, but I don't totally understand why.

We need to know the Creator. We need to know deeply the God who made us, and when we do, the answer to the question of ultimate things comes clearly into focus. You can learn to be yourself. I can learn to be me. I get there when I know God. I know God through his Son, Jesus, and Jesus said, "Then you will know the truth, and the truth will set you free" (John 8:32). We have been set free to live, to *truly* live, but we will only know that freedom when we learn to be who we are. Not a falsely created version designed to manipulate the world around us, but the honest version that reflects the nature and character of God, who has come to live within us through Christ.

Are you searching? At some level, are you trying to *find yourself*? Quit looking for answers apart from God. It's why I wrote this book. *Learning to Be You* is a road map, and I pray that as you work your way through it, you will be reoriented to who you truly are and therein find the true joy and freedom of living that God desires for you to know.

First Things First

1

An Honest Struggle

DO WE KNOW WHO WE REALLY ARE?

For we are God's handiwork, created in Christ Jesus to do good works, which God prepared in advance for us to do.

Ephesians 2:10

We don't know ourselves, we knowledgeable people—we are personally ignorant about ourselves. And there's good reason for that. We've never tried to find out who we are—how could it happen that one day we'd discover ourselves?

Friedrich Nietzsche, *On the Genealogy of Morals*

While thumbing through the pages of *Sports Illustrated* recently, I came across the sad story of one-time tennis prodigy Jennifer Capriati. Groomed for stardom from a very young age, she had risen to the top of the tennis world only to be sidelined by repeated injuries, finally being forced to retire. As she struggled to maintain her place in tennis, she fell into the world of drugs and alcohol, unable to cope with failure. She eventually was hospitalized following a failed suicide attempt, and when reporters questioned her after her release, she said, "It all started to crumble when I quit playing tennis. After that I could not figure out who am I? What am I?"[1]

Capriati's statement was painful in its own right, but what I found particularly stunning was that someone finally had the courage to admit asking the question. She had reached a place in her life where she could articulate the foundation of her problem: she didn't know who she was. Tennis no longer defined her, so she had no answer. While it may sound cliché, it is the question that pounds in the hearts of people all over the world: Who am I, really? In the case of Capriati, her ability to answer that question was a matter of life and death. I suggest the stakes are that high for each of us.

How could they not be? If we don't know our true identity and live out of it, then everything about our lives becomes false—counterfeit. Either we are trying to find out who we really are, or we are living as someone we're not. Both scenarios create tremendous internal conflict and confusion. And when we're confused, we often do things that yield painful consequences.

In May of 1985, I had recently graduated from the Harvard of the South, Southern Methodist University, and had taken a job in personnel and marketing with a computer company in Carrollton, Texas. My role was to attend trade and high-tech shows to market our products and also to help the managers in our company fill their open positions for software engineers and computer programmers. It seemed like a great job to me at the time.

What I did not anticipate, however, was the constant pressure to conform. The behavior of many of my co-workers was often borderline at best. Worst of all was their monthly marketing association luncheons at what is referred to as a "high-end gentlemen's club." I don't think I need to describe it any more than that. Dallas had such clubs all over the place, and many catered to businessmen with expense accounts looking for lavish ways to spend their money and impress their clients. It was quickly made clear to me that I was expected to attend these meetings.

I knew I shouldn't, but my desire to succeed increased the pressure I felt to compromise my standards and beliefs. I couldn't help thinking that I was falling behind others in my office because I was missing out on the information exchanged at these lunches. Finally, and without warning, the situation came to a head. My boss came into my office and said, "David, you've been here almost a year, and you never go with us to our association meetings. You don't know the people, and it's consequently hurting your ability to do your job. What gives?"

It's amazing how many thoughts can run through your head at a moment like that. I am a disciple of Jesus Christ. I am his. Was I going to be that person, or was I going to be a counterfeit? Was I going to be my true self or a false representation? Essentially, was I going to choose to live as a disciple of Jesus Christ *for real*?

I'd like to tell you that I boldly rose from my chair to share the gospel with my boss, but that would be a lie. Lying is generally not a good way to start a book. The truth is that not boldly but meekly I mumbled something about my faith, and not hearing me, my boss said, "What?" Again I fumbled through a few words about what I believe, and miraculously, he got the message. He said something about not realizing the location made me uncomfortable and that he would see about changing it. I could feel the sweat rolling down my back as he left the room—the sheer anxiety of the moment finally starting to dissipate. The apostle Paul I was not, but I got through it. At least I had not been counterfeit, but it was not over.

I immediately feared repercussions, imagining co-workers whispering behind my back, making fun of my convictions, or planning to cut me out of future deals or meetings. But it never happened. To my surprise, I found that others valued me more for having the courage to be who I truly was. Because of their reaction, I found myself standing a bit taller, growing in the confidence of living out of my true self. By God's grace, I had somehow managed to be who I truly was in my faith, and I often think back on the moment, grateful that God allowed me to think it through before I was asked the question.

The reality is that people often don't know who they are, and if they do, they frequently lack the inner resolve to live out of that true identity. As a result, at the first sign of turmoil or pressure, they face enormous internal conflict. The stress and disequilibrium become unbearable because they honestly don't know who they are or what they should do. I have seen it happen frequently in teenagers. I often had students who faithfully attended the youth group I led. They prayed the prayers, read the Scriptures, and earnestly desired to walk with God. Yet on the weekends when they were with their peers, they behaved in ways contrary to their faith in God. Consequently, they went home racked by guilt, confused by their own duplicity, and frustrated at their inability to live out of their true identity in Christ.

The same can be true for adults. On the one hand, a man comes to church with his family, takes part in a small group, and serves on a ministry team. On the other, he swears right along with his co-workers, bends his ethics for personal gain, drinks too heavily, and leers at attractive women. He arrives home at night torn by his duplicity, wondering, "Which man am I really?" He too is racked by guilt. He knows who he is in Christ, but he is not living out of that identity. The longer it continues, the more distant he grows from the true life he yearns for.

Of course, no one is perfect. Regardless of how secure I may be in my true identity, I am going to make mistakes and live out of a false one. Even so, the more we align our behavior with our true identity, the more we will know the abundant life promised by God in John 10:10: "I have come that they may have life, and have it to the full." The more we can live for real, the less time we will spend grinding through feelings of guilt, conflict, and frustration. My prayer is that this book will help you know who you really are and then give you the courage to live out of that true identity. So go ahead. Ask the question.

Who Am I?

We all grapple with this question at some point, and if we don't get the answer right, we will find ourselves grappling with it over and over again. The process seems endless, frustrating. We have various means of answering this question, many of which are culturally or vocationally driven. I am a pastor. I am a banker. I am a student. I am Joe's wife or Betty's husband. I am an activist. I am a vegetarian. I am a quadriplegic. I am an alcoholic. I am a single parent. I am a Democrat or Republican. I am a Gator or a Longhorn. I am nothing. I am everything. I am lost. I am alone. And the list goes on. It's an identity question. In the recession of these past years, with jobs being lost and lives reoriented, it's a question that has wedged its way to the forefront of people's thoughts. Many have been forced to ask, "If I can't keep this job and provide for my family, or continue being a member of the club, or live in this neighborhood, or drive this car, or afford these clothes, or succeed in this relationship, then who am I?"

While we sometimes create elaborate systems to avoid it, it is the drumbeat that echoes out of some deep place in our soul. We want to know the answer, but we're never quite sure how to find it. Regardless, the answer we settle on is vital because it shapes how we see ourselves, and consequently, how we see our world. Did you realize that? How you answer this one question is going to shape nearly every other dimension of your life. If that's the case, then it may be worth the effort to get the answer right.

God's Children

According to our culture, we should know who we are: We are bearers and creators of our own light. We are little gods unto ourselves. We know what is best for us. We know what is true for us. In the words of objectivist philosopher Ayn Rand, "The concept of man is as a heroic being, with his own happiness as the moral purpose of his life, with productive achievement as his noblest activity, and reason as his only absolute."[2] Isn't that it? That's who we are—our own "heroic being" with our own happiness as our only purpose. At least that's what we're told. In the end, however, how could that possibly work? Knowing what I know about myself, my own flaws and failures, how could I ever be the source of my own identity or being? The self is never enough; yet that is the message of our time.

So how do you answer the *who am I* question? Do you define your identity according to your career? Is your sense of self driven solely by your perceived status or reputation? Is your identity grounded in some past success or failure? In an honest examination of your heart, how do you answer?

Thankfully, there is no need to continue searching blindly for an answer. God has given us an enormous piece to the puzzle, and it is found in the gospel. The good news of the gospel, and the purpose of this book, is: (1) to point you to your true identity in Christ, (2) to give you the courage to live out of that identity, and in the process, (3) to quell the internal conflicts that often arise when you cannot do the first two. The answer begins with what God has revealed to us in his Word. Paul writes in Ephesians 1:4–5, "In love [God] predestined us for adoption to sonship through Jesus Christ, in accordance with his pleasure and will."

Let's break that open. In Christ, we are the children of God. In Christ, we have been given all the rights and privileges of being part of God's family. Take that in for a moment. Out of love, the Creator of the universe, and the Creator of your life, has adopted you as his own, thus granting you full inclusion into his family. You are a child of God. You are not *becoming* a child of God or *hoping* you're a child of God or *working* to be a child of God. You *are* a child of God. It is already completed. You're in. Question: Who are you? Answer: You are a child of God.

Harry Greene is the president of Good News Jail and Prison Ministry, an international ministry that places chaplains in jails and prisons around the world. A onetime inmate himself, Harry tells the story of how he found Christ in his jail cell as a result of his relationship with a chaplain. On the day Harry was released, that chaplain took Harry to his home and invited him to live in his basement until he could find suitable work. Even more amazing was this: when it came time for dinner, the chaplain invited Harry to eat with his family. The chaplain's wife, his two daughters, and Harry all sat down together. There was Harry, a convicted felon, a former inmate, eating at the family table! In spite of his past, he had been given all the rights and privileges of being part of that chaplain's family.

That's what it means to be a child of God. You dine at his table. In spite of what you have done or failed to do, you are invited to come and be part of God's eternal family. You are not relegated to the basement. Far from it. God says, "Come, eat at my table. You belong to me. You are my child."

What's more, God cherishes us. Zephaniah 3:17 declares that our God "will rejoice over you with singing." Imagine that. God delights in you so much that he sings about it. Further, God declares through Paul in Ephesians 2:10 that we are the workmanship of God. Our lives have been crafted by the hand of the Master, uniquely and wonderfully made so that we can serve him in building his kingdom. When we lay hold of these truths and internalize them deeply, we are changed. How can we not be? Our lives flow from the hand of our loving Father, and therefore, our identity is found in and through him and him alone. It is a simple yet uniquely powerful truth that can change not only our hearts but also how we see ourselves and how we see the world.

Inner Conflict

As powerful as that may be, this is a truth that often escapes us. This is either because we do not grasp the Father's character, nature, and love or because we become stuck in the mold into which our culture is trying to force us.

Just as we considered the life of Jennifer Capriati at the beginning of the chapter, let's consider the life of another young woman. She says she is a follower of Jesus Christ. She tells me her faith is deep and that it is only through God's love that she can make it from day to day. But each week, even though she has been to church, she finds the pressure to conform to the expectations of others so strong that she cannot withstand it. She binge drinks. She has sex with multiple partners. She smokes pot. Her fear of being rejected by her peers is so strong that she cannot live out of her true identity in Christ. The result, of course, is that she returns home and spends the next day awash in guilt over having failed to live for Christ. She knows who she is, but she does not live out of that identity. Two totally different scenarios, but both resulted in deep internal pain. Jennifer Capriati didn't know who she was apart from tennis. She had no answer, and the internal pain drove her to try to end her life. Another woman knows who she is, but she can't actually bring herself to live that way. The internal conflicts that both these women faced are similarly rooted in the question of personal identity—a question so seldom understood but one that is ultimately answered in Christ.

This inner conflict is something we all struggle with, even when we are *in* Christ. Paul, one of the great leaders in the early church and author of much of the New Testament, writes these words in Romans 7:15: "I do not understand what I do. For what I want to do I do not do, but what I hate I do."

I think that describes it quite well for all of us. We know what we want to do. We often know what we should do. Yet we wind up doing the very opposite, and those decisions drive us crazy. Why am I acting this way? Why did I just do that? It is part of being human, part of the struggle of every human heart. There is inner conflict in regard to our choices, and we yearn to know how to find peace. We yearn to live as we truly are and not some counterfeit we have created.

Miraculously, God has even given us an internal instinct to try to solve this problem. In his infinite and eternal knowledge, he knew we would try to form our identity through the things of this world. So he gave us an internal mechanism to counteract our natural instincts. God reveals this through Solomon in Ecclesiastes 3:11: "[God] has also set eternity in the human heart."

The Faint Whisper

How cool is that? Within each of us God has planted the question of ultimate things. That's what *eternity* means. He has set within our hearts a desire to understand what is truly eternal, or in other words, what truly matters. This desire makes us search to know who we truly are and how we fit in this world. It is that internal, God-given mechanism that drives us to search until we find the answer that satisfies the deepest yearnings of our hearts. It's like a homing device. We may not know why, but we have this deep desire within us that makes us search for the way to our heart's true home: the joy of a deep relationship with our Maker. I love the fact that God did not leave us to our own devices. He knew we would often choose to follow false paths, so he graciously gave us a tool that keeps us searching, looking, asking—until that day when we are finally led back to him. He has set eternity in our hearts.

Thomas Kelly, a renowned Quaker teacher and author from the mid-1900s, writes in his book *A Testament of Devotion*:

> Over the margins of life comes a whisper, a faint call, a premonition of richer living which we know we are passing by. Strained by the very mad pace of our daily outer burdens, we are further strained by an inward uneasiness, because we have hints that there is a way of life vastly richer and deeper

than all this hurried existence, a life of unhurried serenity and peace and power.[3]

That's it, isn't it? That's the question of eternity in our hearts. It's that nagging feeling, that gaping hole, that emptiness you can't put your finger on, or as Kelly says, that "faint whisper." It's the question of ultimate, eternal things: Who am I and what am I doing here? It's always there. Sometimes whispering, sometimes banging, it's always there. We often can't explain why we feel the way we do, but we hear the whisper that there must be more to this life than we are experiencing. We believe that somehow we are more than just the sum of our relationships or the value of our paycheck. We want to know, but it's a struggle to discover. And sometimes, even when we do discover it, we are pressured to live out of a counterfeit identity instead of our true identity in Christ.

The answer to our struggle, the answer to our inner conflict, is found in the life of a Jewish carpenter who—when he is known to you—changes not only how you see yourself but also how you engage your world as you live out of your true identity. Ravi Zacharias writes in *Has Christianity Failed You?*:

> What do we know about ourselves? We know what we feel, what we long for, whom we love, hate, judge. In short, everything we know about ourselves, we know through our senses. But still, our knowledge of ourselves is partial. God is the only one who knows us comprehensively. By denying Him and His existence, we reject the one person who knows us completely, with the result that we truly become strangers to ourselves and to others.[4]

A builder who painstakingly constructs every element of his own home is going to know that home better than anyone else. Why would we dare to assume that we know more about ourselves than the one who made us? That is contrary to logic. If God made us, then *of course* he knows us inside and out. Psalm 139:1–4 reminds us:

> You have searched me, LORD,
> and you know me.
> You know when I sit and when I rise;
> you perceive my thoughts from afar.
> You discern my going out and my lying down;
> you are familiar with all my ways.
> Before a word is on my tongue
> you, LORD, know it completely.

I am living my life within the parameters of how I have been made and who God has made me to be, but I did not make myself. God did. Thus if I am uncertain about who I am or how I fit into this world or why I have certain gifts or qualities and not others, my most effective recourse is to seek the Maker. I need to quiz the one who made me. In fact, I need to do more than just ask questions. I need to actually *know* the Maker. When I know the Maker, then I will understand his purpose in making me. I will become familiar with his patterns and habits in how he relates not only to me but also to all of those he has made.

But That's Not Me

In my more than twenty years of pastoral ministry, I have encountered many people who daily live in a gray fog of uncertainty about who they really are. And I had some years when I lived in that fog myself. When people don't know who they are, their lack of clarity produces decisions and behaviors that are destructive not only to themselves but also to those around them. The evidence for this truth is found in the number of times we hear people say, "But that's not me."

I saw it again recently when a well-known football player was suspended for several games because of his arrest for domestic violence. When he returned, he stood before the microphones and said, "I am glad to be back. I know what I did was wrong, but the person who did that—that's not me. It's just not me." When people make such a statement, what they are essentially saying is: "That behavior was not indicative of my true identity. My true identity is something else. I am not what I did." They know it, but they can't find their way forward. They are not defined by their past actions, but if they're not, then what does define them? What is their true identity? That's what I always want to ask the unfaithful husband: If that's not you, fine, but can you tell me who you really are?

I pray that this book will point you to the answer. Whether you are someone who has never known God and thus been unable to truly know yourself, or you know God but have never been able to live out of your true nature, feeling the stress and turmoil of deep inner conflict, there is an answer. It is found in God, and it will change your life. Part 1 will establish our struggle with the identity question and our need to know God in order to find the answer. Part 2 will look at the attributes of God and how our understanding of those attributes shapes our personal identity. God is not some distant, other-worldly being. God is the one who has come to reside *in us* by faith. God is the one who has created us in his image. Therefore, as I understand who God is, I understand how and for what purpose he has made me. As I understand the attributes of God, I learn the true attributes of myself. By knowing them, I can reshape my identity into the one that is eternally true instead of the counterfeit identity thrust on me by the world. God's nature reveals our true identity; therefore, let's explore what his nature reveals.

It's easy for us to say, "But that's not me." The harder, more challenging part is to follow where that statement leads and discover who we really are (as we'll explore more in part 3). I pray you'll take that journey with me.

2

A God We Can Know

GETTING ACQUAINTED WITH A GOD
WHO IS NEARER THAN WE EVER DREAMED

The highest science, the loftiest speculation, the mightiest philosophy, which can ever engage the attention of a child of God, is the name, the nature, the person, the work, the doings, and the existence of the great God whom he calls his Father.

C. H. Spurgeon

Let not the wise boast of their wisdom or the strong boast of their strength or the rich boast of their riches, but let the one who boasts boast about this: that they have the understanding to know me.

Jeremiah 9:23–24

For as long as I can remember, I have had control issues. Yes, I admit it. I don't like being in an environment over which I don't have at least some measure of control. I don't like being in situations where I feel trapped: packed elevators, overcrowded restaurants, or, in the case I want to tell you about, MRI tubes.

Five years ago when I was having trouble with the nerves in my arm, a doctor in Dallas said I needed an MRI. Needless to say, I was not happy about that. The thought of spending ninety minutes in a small tube made my head feel like it was going to explode. I would be trapped with no means of control! When I shared that with the doctor, he said, "No worries. I'll give you some medicine for that." So I showed up on the day of the test, and the nurse gave me two little pills with a glass of water. I didn't bother to ask what they were, but by the time I went for the test, I felt fabulous! I got into that tube without a care in the world. The technicians tuned the radio to ESPN Sports (who knew they had speakers in MRI tubes!). I was laughing and joking with the technician over the intercom, and the ninety-minute process flew by. When it was over, my dad took me to my favorite southern-cooking restaurant where we got a big bag of fried chicken to go. I got home, ate my chicken, reviewed my experience with Leigh, and went to bed.

The odd thing about the whole experience was that when I woke up the next morning, I remembered a number of things about the previous day, but it seemed like it hadn't really happened. My memories had an odd, dreamlike quality. My mind was so hazy and fuzzy that I woke Leigh (she *loves* being awakened early) and asked her, "Did I have my MRI yesterday?" When I went down to get my coffee, I started going through the trash to find evidence from the night before that I had, in fact, eaten fried chicken. I wasn't convinced that I had actually done that. Needless to say, when I got the bill in the mail, I was fully convinced. Obviously, there was something in those tiny pills!

We have all had moments like that. Things happen and we know they've happened, but for some reason our memories begin to fade or we start to doubt their veracity. We have a conversation; we share an experience; we encounter a person—we know it happened, but the further we get from the experience, the less sure we are of what actually took place. In so many ways, I think that's where we can find ourselves in our spiritual lives. We grapple to understand our own identity and how we fit in the world, and in that process, we may think about God. We may even have moments with God—experiences in which we think God is near. The further we get from them, however, or the more we think about them, the more we wonder: Did that happen? Was that real? Was that a dream? Was God really there, or was that last night's pizza? At some point, I think everyone asks himself or herself: Who is God, and is he real?

There was a time, though, when that question was never asked. In Genesis, Adam and Eve never asked if God was real. They knew he was real because he was right there with them. They didn't have to ask; they knew. But then what happened? God's people rebelled. They separated themselves from God, and as the consequences of that decision sank in, they found themselves further and further away. People no longer saw him or heard him in the same way, and even though God sent messengers from time to time, they were so unfamiliar with his voice that they doubted it was really his. They built towers trying to get to him.

Occasionally, they had experiences of him, but more and more they doubted. They questioned. Essentially, that's the point we have reached today. God's cultural absence is so great and any acknowledgment of him so removed that we wonder if our prior thoughts of God or experiences with him really happened at all. We wonder if God is actually real and at work in our lives. "Did I ever know God, or was it all some sort of dream?" Bill Bright asks the question for us: "Is it possible for a mere human, less than a tiny speck on the pebble of a planet in the midst of a vast galaxy, to know the great God who created everything?"[1] That eternal question in our hearts won't leave us alone, so what do we do? Much like I did the day after my MRI, we ask questions. We go through the trash, looking for evidence of what we think is true but are not quite sure of. And when we do that, what do we find?

We find the voices of hundreds in our culture eager to line up and tell us, "Your hunch is right. It's a dream. God is in your head. You made him up." We hear voices like Samuel Harris in *Letter to a Christian Nation*: "I have set out to demolish the intellectual and moral pretensions of Christianity in its most committed forms."[2] We hear Richard Dawkins in *The God Delusion*: "The God of the Old Testament is arguably the most unpleasant character in all fiction: a petty, unjust, unforgiving control freak."[3] We hear Christopher Hitchens in *God Is Not Great: How Religion Poisons Everything*.[4] These are not fringe books. All three have been on the *New York Times* bestseller list. These are the voices that people are listening to, and for many, they only confirm the nagging questions we have: Is God real? Can I know him? According to many, the answer is: No, you can't. No, he's not real.

Even so, I think these authors have done us a favor, because they have created a cultural conversation about God. Because these militant atheists have made their negative views about God so blunt and aggressive, people have been forced to consider whether those views are correct. In many ways, it is the drumbeat of the current cultural conversation. Many have an increased interest in spiritual things, but they're not quite sure how to answer. It's like a buffet. They try every-thing. Well, let's look at that. If we cannot know ourselves until we know God, then we have to ask: Can we actually know God, and if so, how?

In exploring this question, John 16 provides some helpful answers. Jesus is talking to the disciples about how radically their lives are going to change when he leaves. Up to that point, their world had been fairly stable. Jesus called them; they obediently followed. They heard him teach and saw the impact he had on others, but the closer Jesus got to Jerusalem, the more things started to change. Opposition grew. Things were not as peaceful, and then Jesus started talking about his departure. He mentioned his coming death and that the disciples would endure similar persecution and suffering. The entirety of their lives was based on this relationship with Jesus, so at this point the disciples were probably wondering some of the very same questions I have raised here: Jesus, are you the person we thought you were? Were the past three years just an illusion, or was this whole thing with you—and with God—real? Thankfully, Jesus recognized their fears and their doubts, and he taught in regard to those questions.

A Knowable God

Initially, here's where we can find great confidence: we can know God because God wants to be known. Jesus says the Holy Spirit "will bring glory to me by taking what is mine and making it known to you" (John 16:14 NIV 1984). He says in Matthew 7:8 that everyone who seeks will find. Does that sound like a God who is trying to hide? I think not. Who is Jesus? He is the greatest single, personal revelation of the living God—God in human flesh—God speaking his desire for us to know him.

Further, if there is a Creator who has no beginning and no end, who set forth the heavens and the earth, and who continues to sustain the universe as we know it, then it stands to reason that we can never know that Creator unless he chooses to be known. If God wanted to remain hidden, he could have. If he is truly God, he has no need of us. He did not need us for love or survival or function. If he wanted to remain hidden and unknown, he could have chosen that course. Yet that's not what he did. God created, and that creation allows us a general knowledge of who he is.

So if that's the case, then don't you want to explore that? If it is possible for you to know the one who not only made the universe but also made you, don't you think that is worthy of your time and investment? Knowing God should be our primary purpose in life. Yet amazingly, the vast majority give it only a cursory glance. J. I. Packer writes in *Knowing God*, "What were we made for? To know God. What aim should we set ourselves in life? To know God. What is the best thing in life, bringing more joy, delight and contentment, than anything else? The knowledge of God."[5]

Jesus says, "This is eternal life: that they know you" (John 17:3). In the final analysis, our internal yearning to understand who we really are flows from our desire to know true life. We want our lives to matter. We want to believe there is a reason for our existence. When we know who made us, and therein understand our purpose, the doors to knowing ourselves fly wide open. If you think about it, everything we do, think, say, and believe in life is guided by what we think about or believe about God. Bill Bright writes, "What we believe to be true about God's character affects our friendships, our work, our leisure. . . . Because of the wrong view of God in our culture today, our society is in moral turmoil, and we are in danger of losing our moral soul."[6]

I believe there is a link between the declining trajectory of our culture and the distance we have put between ourselves and God. Distance makes relationships harder. When I first began my relationship with Leigh, we lived two hundred miles apart. We had to navigate that distance for two years before we ever lived in the same city. We loved each other and were committed to each other, but it was difficult and painful. The distance made communication more challenging, and those challenges led to cracks and fissures in the relationship—cracks that would never have happened had we been in each other's presence.

The same is true in our relationship with God. Distance creates problems. We have kept him at arm's length, and we are reaping the harvest of that distance. The only way we are going to find our true selves and true life is through knowing God. We need to draw close to him. If you want to find meaning in life, if you want to make sense of the world, if you want to find answers to the problems you face, all this is related to and tied up in your knowledge of God. It is the most important pursuit of our lives and one that leads to a life-changing discovery.

Glory

Have you ever noticed that when you are in the presence of greatness you don't feel so good about yourself? I'll never forget a chance flight I shared with Dr. Billy Graham on a private plane. He shared stories about his crusades at Madison Square Garden (nightly for sixteen weeks), his foray into Russia to share the gospel (millions heard and saw him preach on government-run channel 1), and the fact that he had never asked for money in all his years of ministry. God just provided. He spoke with humble gratitude and not the slightest hint of arrogance. It was just what God had done. Yet as I listened to him, I thought to myself, *My goodness, Swanson, you are a loser. You're a lousy pastor in a small church who can't even figure out how to grow worship attendance.* While not exactly godly thoughts, it was my honest human reaction. Being around Billy Graham gave me a total inferiority complex.

Actually, that's quite common, and I hope that's exactly what happens to us when we begin to grow in our knowledge of God. If we are to ever know who we truly are, we must understand our identity in light of who God is—and God is nothing like us. He is light and glory and holiness. Last time I checked, I am none of those things. The perfection of God's nature informs the imperfection of my own. It tells me who I truly am and reveals my desperate need for a savior. Here's the reality: If you don't grasp how truly bad the bad news is, then you'll never know how really good the Good News is. Before you can understand your true identity, you have to understand God's glory and, as a result, your sinfulness.

Sadly, however, as we have moved God to the edges of our experience, we have reduced him in stature and nature. No longer authoritative, God has become the grandfather in the rocking chair, lovingly winking at us as we wander off in mischief, fully aware that he doesn't have the power to stop us. We have brought him down to our level and enclosed him in a case of our making. Consequently, we believe that somehow God exists to meet our needs and endorse our desires, flawed though they may be. Any true knowledge of God, however, must begin with his essential nature—a nature contained in one word: *glory*.

Over and over again, as God reveals himself in Scripture, what we find is *glory*. Psalm 19:1 reminds us, "The heavens declare the glory of God." Ezekiel encounters God and says,

"This was the appearance of the likeness of the glory of the Lord. When I saw it, I fell facedown" (Ezek. 1:28). At the moment of his calling, Isaiah said, "I saw the Lord, high and exalted, seated on a throne; and the train of his robe filled the temple. . . . 'Woe to me!' I cried. 'I am ruined! For I am a man of unclean lips'" (Isa. 6:1, 5). The great hymn by Walter Smith uses these words: "Immortal, invisible, God only wise, in light inaccessible hid from our eyes." What is that light? It is his glory. We must know that first. He is not a meek grandfather figure whom we control. This is God as he truly is—veiled in light so bright and glorious that he is inaccessible to the human eye! It is hard for us to even imagine such glory, but it is true.

In Exodus 33, Moses prays a dangerous prayer, and God answers it. He does not ask God to change his circumstances. He does not ask God, as we so often do, to solve his problems. He does not present God with a list of needs to take care of. Instead, he prays, "Now show me your glory" (Exod. 33:18). In other words, "God, I just want *you*. Show me *you*. Let me know *you*." And that's exactly what God did. He said, "I will cause all my goodness to pass in front of you. . . . But . . . you cannot see my face, for no one may see me and live. . . . When my glory passes by, I will put you in a cleft in the rock and cover you with my hand until I have passed by" (Exod. 33:19–22).

Did you catch that? Does that sound like a God to whom we dictate? Does that sound like a God who can be kept in a box of our making? We cannot see this God and live. Understand this: were the fullness of God's glorious presence to enter your room, you would be destroyed by the sheer magnitude of who he is. Even so, we walk around as if God is contained—limited—controlled. It's why we can take his name in vain without giving it another thought—why we can enter worship without any sense of expectation—why we encounter trouble with only anxious foreboding. We don't know who we're dealing with. The reality of God is *glory*.

Glory Revealed

Were that the end of the story, we would all be in trouble. We could never reach such a God of glory. We could never be in relationship with him. As I have been saying, however, while God *is* glorious, he also wants to be known. Thus his glory is revealed. John 1:14 says, "The Word became flesh and dwelt among us, and we beheld His glory, the glory as of the only begotten of the Father, full of grace and truth" (NKJV). When God took on human flesh in Jesus Christ, glory came down. The glory of God was there for us to see. Thus if you want to know the glory of God, then you need to know Jesus. And here's the incredible part: God is glorious. He has revealed that glory in Jesus. When we invite Jesus to enter our lives, the wonder of God's glory comes to take up residence in us. Now to be sure, it is not the fullness of that glory, but there is a glimpse, a taste, a foreshadowing of what we will one day know in full. Through Christ, God's glory comes to dwell in us.

If that's the case, then what do you assume is naturally going to happen? God's glory is going to start seeping out of our lives because *that's who we are*. Let me explain. In Exodus 34:35, when Moses came off the mountain after having been in the presence of God, we are told his face was "radiant." In fact, it was so radiant that he had to wear a veil to cover it in the presence of the people. By the Spirit, Christ, who lives in the glory of the Father, has come to live in us. So Paul writes, "And we all, who with unveiled faces contemplate the Lord's glory, are being transformed into his image with ever-increasing glory, which comes from the Lord" (2 Cor. 3:18).

Wow. God is glorious. His glory is revealed in Christ. Christ lives in us. As a result, when we live obediently in that knowledge, God's glory comes pouring out of us. How could it not? If God's glory is in us, then it is naturally going to start coming out of our pores, and as with Moses, it's going to be so evident that people will ask, "What happened to you?" And that is one of the true joys of being a pastor: I have seen God's glory on the faces of those whose hearts follow after God. I have seen his glory on the face of a young woman in our church who decided to quit her job and give up her comfortable life in Orlando to move to Haiti and serve people ravaged by natural disasters and cholera. To see her face when she describes those she serves is to see the glory of God. I feel I could reach out and touch it with my finger. I have seen God's glory on the face of a dying man, a man full of faith and love for God, describing what he sees as he prepares to enter into God's glory. I almost wanted to go with him. I have seen God's glory when my firstborn child, cord wrapped around his neck, was quickly removed from my wife, blue and not breathing, only to have him put in my lap minutes later, crying and wonderfully alive. I have seen God's glory in the face of a child who is disabled and unable to engage his world in the same manner as most children but who has discovered that he is loved.

There is only one way to describe it. *Glory*. And it is around us every day. It is in us through Christ.

Do you see why this is so important? We must know God to know ourselves, and we must know God as he is, not some culturally conditioned counterfeit, because who he is tells us who we are. You and I—through Christ—are the living, breathing bearers of the glory of God. Sinful and imperfect?

Yes. But his glory is there, and he wants it to be reflected in us and on us. Talk about good news. I'm not who I once was. I am not defined by my past, by what I have done, or by what I have failed to do. I am defined by the one who lives in me, by his wondrous, glorious presence.

Not All at Once

Before you get too excited about all this, let me remind you how our relationship with God works. I think sometimes we get too accustomed to having whatever we want whenever we want it and in ample supply. Technology has advanced to the point that we get information and answers instantly. This is not the case with God. It can't be—we could not bear it. Jesus says in John 16:12, "I have much more to say to you, more than you can now bear." In other words, there are things he will eventually show us that we could not understand right now.

As finite human beings, how can we possibly understand the fullness of the one who is infinite in nature? We can't. God does reveal himself, but he does so gradually. Paul gives a great description of this in 1 Corinthians 3 when he paints the picture of a maturing child. At first we drink milk, because milk is all we can handle. As we grow, however, we become ready for solid food. Are you going to make your teenage daughter the CEO of your company tomorrow? Of course not. She wouldn't be ready for that. But as she matures, you can teach her new elements and dimensions of your business.

God acts in our lives in precisely the same manner. So like Moses and Paul, we should hunger after more of God. In your pursuit of God, are you still immature and feeding on milk, or have you started to live faithfully and obediently so that you are ready for more solid food? Again, the more you know of the glorious nature of God, the more you grasp your identity as his glorious child. The two are indelibly linked. However, the more you know, the more you also realize how little you know of the infinite, immeasurable God. Even so, this study is worth our time and effort, because our knowledge of God is what determines how we see and understand ourselves and everything else in life.

The knowledge of God must begin with his glory. He wants to be known, and the clues are everywhere if we'll just look. I came across just such a clue not long ago when I heard speaker Louie Giglio describe a wonderful part of the human body called *laminin*. Without getting into all the technical jargon of molecular biology, laminin is the cell adhesion molecule. The human body is organized around various types of cells, each of which has a different job or purpose. But what holds them all together? Why doesn't our body just fall apart? Answer: laminin. Laminin is the glue, so to speak, the entity that keeps the core elements of our body together so we can live and function in the way God designed.

You may be thinking, *Well, three cheers for laminin*. But have you ever seen a picture of a cell model of laminin? In all its scientific glory, it's a cross. A cross. Colossians 1:17 says, "He is before all things, and in him all things hold together." Our God, revealed in Christ, holds all things together in his hands. Our knowledge of that truth is most clearly revealed on the cross of Christ. And what holds the human body together? Laminin. And what does it look like? A cross. Coincidence? Some would say yes, but I think it is yet another way God reveals his glory to us. I think God is the one who holds all things together—our bodies—our world—our lives. And the only way we will ever find redemption is in the knowledge of God and a right relationship with him. He is at the core of all things, creating, sustaining, and redeeming—holding us together for his glory. Let's seek to know him, and through knowing him, may we come to know who we truly are. If God is at the core of our physical nature, revealed in a little thing like laminin, then God is the core of our identity as well.

3

Hide and Seek

WHY WE RUN FROM BEING KNOWN

Then the man and his wife heard the sound of the LORD God as he was walking in the garden in the cool of the day, and they hid from the LORD God among the trees of the garden. But the LORD God called out to the man, "Where are you?"

Genesis 3:8–9

Most men lead lives of quiet desperation and go to the grave with the song still in them.

Henry David Thoreau

Hide and seek. It's such a great game, and it's almost universal. I imagine most people around the world know something about this game. I played it with my children when they were young, and I noticed something as the years went by: the older they got, the more skilled they became at hiding. When they were little, they crouched down behind the sofa and laughed the whole time, giving themselves away. But as they got older, they got harder and harder to find. They buried themselves beneath mounds of clothing in a closet or folded their little bodies into a crevice behind a piece of furniture. And yes, I'll admit it: the time came when I could not find them at all. Their hiding places were simply too good.

In fact, playing that game led to one of the scarier moments in my life. It was about two in the afternoon, and I was working in my office when I got a phone call. (This was back when cell phones were in a bag that weighed five pounds and stayed in your car.) I picked up the receiver and said hello, but there was no response from the other end. Instead, I heard the faint but frantic voice of my wife describing the clothing that our little three-year-old girl, Kaylee, was wearing. Then I heard a male voice ask, "And when was the last time you saw her?" At that point, I dropped the phone and ran to my car, driving home as fast as I could. I arrived ten minutes later to find a scene that felt like it belonged in a movie. Two police cars and three fire trucks, lights on, were in my driveway and yard. Police officers and firefighters fanned out, meticulously searching a ravine covered in ivy that was directly across the street from our house. Neighbors were all over the block, looking in bushes and rain-filled gullies. And my wife stood in the driveway, her frozen, tearstained face staring numbly forward.

I ran up to her and asked, "What in the world is happening?" She buried her head in my shoulder and said, "I can't find her. I've looked everywhere, and I can't find her." Kaylee had not been seen for more than two hours. The police had informed my wife that with each hour that passed, the odds of a happy ending decreased. Now I was frantic. I talked to the officers and got my wife to tell me the exact details of when she last saw Kaylee, and then I started searching. Believing that she might come to the sound of my voice, I began yelling her name at the top of my lungs as I walked all over our neighborhood. Nothing.

Then I decided to start from the beginning. I went back to our house and started searching each room, again calling her name as loudly as I could. Then it hit me. Hide and seek. I had been home at lunch that day, and we had played hide and seek, so I decided to check her favorite hiding spots. I went into her bedroom and pulled back the long, flowing drapes. Sure enough, there she was at the base of the curtains, curled up in a ball, sound asleep. My heart leaped. I grabbed her, crying and saying over and over again, "Kaylee! Kaylee, I found you!" I rushed outside, clutching her in my arms, shouting to all the people in my yard. Cheers went up. I'm not sure I have ever had a more euphoric moment in my life. As I looked at my precious little girl, I tried to explain to her why all the people were in our yard and why all the police cars were there. "Kaylee, we couldn't find you, and all these people came to help us look for you." "But Daddy," she said, "I wasn't lost. I was just hiding."

I'll never forget it. What a day, but what a lesson too. That experience reinforced a deep truth about who I am as a human being. It helped me understand one of the essential elements of my identity: I like to hide. We all do. We hide from others, we hide from ourselves, and we hide from God. While God wants to be known and is constantly trying to reveal himself to us, we are often the opposite. We tend to hide. If we are ever going to live for real—if we are ever going to live as we truly are—then we need to understand that dynamic so we can move from living falsely—hiding our true selves—to living authentically in Christ. So if God wants to be known, why is it that we want to hide?

Our True Nature

Genesis 2–3 paints the picture for us quite well: Adam and Eve have been given a good life by God. They have a great place to live. Good jobs. Happy marriage. No stress. The only thing they can't do is eat the fruit from a tree in the middle of the garden. Not a bad life. I think I'd sign up for that. Even so, the serpent comes and tempts them, saying, "When you eat from it your eyes will be opened, and you will be like God" (Gen. 3:5). And there it is. The root of our nature is one that always wants to be "like God." We want to be our own god. We want to be the one who calls the shots, dictates the outcomes, and makes the decisions. We want to follow our own desires without judgment or delay. We earnestly believe that when it comes to matters of our personal lives, we know best.

While that sounds good on the surface, where does it lead us? It leads us to the very place where we find Adam and Eve in Genesis 3:8, pathetically crouched down behind some bushes hiding from God. They realize their disobedience has broken their relationship with God. They no longer live in the freedom of being who they truly are as children of God. Instead, they are hiding, disconnected from the source of their true selves.

Sadly, we see the evidence of this truth around us each day. People want to live for themselves, and living out of that false identity always leads to hiding. It seems that even with all we have, we always want more. We are never content—never satisfied. Daniel Pink writes in his book *A Whole New Mind*:

Abundance has brought beautiful things to our lives, but that bevy of material goods has not necessarily made us much happier. The paradox of prosperity is that while living standards have risen steadily decade after decade, personal, family and life satisfaction haven't budged."[1]

We never have enough, do we?

- Bernie Madoff built an elaborate Ponzi scheme, stealing money from his clients while hiding the ruse from even his closest associates. Eventually they found his hiding place.
- Mark Sanford, the governor of South Carolina and an outspoken Christian, decided he was in love with a woman in Argentina and made repeated visits to see her. He hid it from his wife and from his constituents. Eventually they found his hiding place.
- Elliott Spitzer, while governor of New York, hid his visits to a prostitution service called Emperor's Club VIP. Eventually they found his hiding place.
- Ted Haggard, pastor of a Colorado megachurch, hid his three-year relationship with another man. Eventually they found his hiding place.

We love to point the finger at these well-known people as if we are somehow better than them, but the sad reality is that we're not. We're all hiders. We all have a human nature that wants to reject the lordship of Jesus Christ in our lives and embrace the pursuit of our own ends. When we do that, we find ourselves in places of shame and denial. The shame and denial then create our need to either hide or pursue our own ends more robustly, desperately hoping that one day they will satisfy. Ultimately, they never do.

The reality is that we're a mess. We can't possibly keep the standard set out by God in his law, and the principles of the world aren't going to satisfy either. Sure, we can insist we're basically good and that it's all going to work out. However, such claims of goodness use the wrong standard. The standard that determines our readiness for entrance into God's eternal kingdom is *not* how we stack up with other human beings. The standard is nothing less than the holiness of God. God said, "Be holy, because I am holy" (1 Peter 1:16). We love to look around and decide that, in comparison to others, we're quite good. Using others to determine the state of our righteousness before God is a faulty standard. Each one of us has a human nature that wants to be our own god, and consequently, to hide from the living God. Each one of us falls short of the holiness of God. Thus, we need a Savior. We need an answer. You can choose to deny that truth, but eventually, you're going to come right back to this very spot. We will always find ourselves hiding, and our hiding places will always be found.

Fighting Our Fear

There's another reason we hide: *fear*. Deep in our gut, we know we are imperfect and broken. We know we make mistakes and poor choices, but at the same time, we work very hard to make sure other people don't know that. Why? We are afraid that if people really know who we are they won't like us. So we hide our true selves and our true issues in favor of a photoshopped version of the real deal. Isn't that an amazing tool? Photoshop has revolutionized photography in such a way that I have to wonder whether what I am looking at is real or only a fixed-up version of the person.

Several years ago, an Orlando TV station reported a controversy unfolding at a local elementary school. A mother was convinced her daughter's yearbook photo had been digitally altered to make her appear to be other than who she was. (Naturally, the mother thought the altered version was unflattering.) The photographer insisted no photoshopping had occurred. So who was right?[2] Countless magazine covers leave us wondering the same thing: Is that the real celebrity or an enhanced version?

In fact, the photoshopping trend became so prevalent that Kathie Lee Gifford and Hoda Kotb, late morning hosts on *Today* on NBC, decided to take the drastic step of doing the show with no makeup. They went on the air *looking the way they truly are*. It was revolutionary. It was hailed as groundbreaking. Other networks actually covered the event. It inspired all kinds of blogs and articles in women's magazines extolling the virtue of *true beauty*. I watched it, and honestly, it was shocking. Like everyone else, I had grown so accustomed to seeing the made-up version of these women that the unadorned version was glaringly different.

We all put on a face to the outside world that covers up the reality of our true selves. Who we are inside is not as attractive as the external version of ourselves, and consequently, our deep fear is that if people know the true version, they will reject us. They will not find us attractive.

John Powell wrote a wonderful book in 1969 entitled *Why Am I Afraid to Tell You Who I Am?* He writes, "I am afraid to tell you who I am, because, if I tell you who I am, you may not like who I am, and it's all that I have."[3] Don't we all know that feeling? I know I do. Yes, I'm a pastor. Yes, I love the Lord. But I too do a lot of hiding, and I too am afraid that if you discover who I truly am, you may not like the real me. So every Sunday morning, while I know I am called by God to preach, there is a small part of me that pushes me to do well so that people will like me. I want them to think I'm okay. I want them to embrace me. I am human, and I want to be loved.

Thus I hide my dark side and work hard to create an image of me that you'll like. It's just part of my human nature—a nature I need to understand if I am going to live out of my true identity instead of the false one I want to hide behind.

Our Pursuer

Were we to stop here, the news would be quite bad. Thankfully, that's not the end of the story. While it is in our nature to hide, the hope of the gospel is that we have a pursuer who is doing all he can to find our hiding places in order to bring us out into the warmth of his light. It's why I find Genesis 3:9 one of the most hopeful and inspiring verses in the Bible. It tells me an enormous amount about myself and God. Adam and Eve are hiding, and God asks a simple question: "Where are you?" Don't you love that? God is trying to find them—and he's trying to find us.

When Adam and Eve try to hide from God, he is aware of it. I am also quite sure he knew what they had done. He told them what the consequences of such a decision would be: *death*. But we don't find him charging through the garden shouting, "Adam and Eve, I'm going to kill you!" No, we find a God of grace and compassion who is ultimately concerned about their relationship with him. He wants to find them because he knows something is wrong. He wants to find them because he loves them. When all is said and done, I know that's one of the deepest longings of my heart. I want to know that I am loved. I want to be pursued. I want to know that when I am lost, someone will care enough about me to come find me. I want to know that when I am hiding, someone will care enough about me to notice that I am missing and go looking for me. Put in its simplest form, I want to be found—and that's exactly what God does.

In and through his love expressed for us in Christ, God graciously draws us out of our hiding places, out of our shame and darkness, and he tells us what we so desperately long to hear: that he knows everything there is to know about us and yet still loves us. Paul writes in Romans 5:8, "But God demonstrates his own love for us in this: While we were still sinners, Christ died for us." While we were still a mess, still in darkness, still hiding, Christ died for us, and that is the greatest expression of God's love. His love begins to pull us out of our hiding places, and we begin to lead authentic lives that reveal our true identity as his children. Yes, we are more deeply stained and darkened by sin than we ever realized, but that is what keeps us humble and empathetic toward our fellow human beings. We know they are in need of the same grace and redemption we are. But in that knowledge, we also realize that we are more cherished, more adored, more treasured, and more loved by God than we ever dared hope.

God knows me as I truly am and loves me anyway. And not only does he love me, but he is willing to sacrifice his life for mine in order that I may live. When I allow that truth to seep into my heart and soul, an amazing transformation begins to happen. I am less concerned about what others think because I know what God thinks. I am less concerned about creating a false identity, but instead, I want to honor God's love by living out of my true identity found in him. I don't have to manipulate others in order to get what I need. I have what I need because I have been eternally and graciously loved by God in Christ. Do you see?

I'll never forget the day Dr. George Hyer, professor of systematic theology at Austin Presbyterian Theological Seminary, stopped me after class and asked, "David, would you be interested in serving as my teaching assistant this semester?" I'm sure I had a look on my face that betrayed my actual feelings. I was dumbfounded. I did not feel particularly good about myself at the time, I was not excelling academically, I was battling anxiety on a daily basis, and I was questioning whether ministry was my true calling. Then this respected professor asked me to work with him. I thought, *Maybe he sees something in me I can't see. He's a smart guy, and he must think I can do it, so maybe I can!* I said yes, and the experience was life changing. I had it in me all along. I just needed someone else to show me what was already there. That's what happens when we draw near to God. He shows us what's already there.

This is the path toward *learning to be you.* The closer we draw to God, the more we will understand his love for us. The more we understand his love for us, the more we understand our true identity as his children. The more we understand our true identity as children of God, the more our lives will authentically reflect that externally. Our external selves will become a more accurate reflection of our internal selves, and along with that comes less internal conflict and less guilt about our choices and decisions. We know who we are. We like who we are, so we live that way. It's a powerful transformation but also a gradual one. Don't expect it to happen all at once. You'll never do it perfectly this side of heaven, but great joy is found when your heart is transformed more and more into his likeness.

An Odd Preference

I will deal with this more fully later in the book, but I want to be careful not to create an unrealistic expectation. Living *authentically* is something we grow in as we grow in Christ, but we still battle that part of ourselves that wants to hide. I love the Lord, but I also know that I still have hiding places—dark places in my heart that need God's light. Remember what happened when God brought Israel out of slavery in Egypt. Before reaching the Promised Land, the people grumbled. "'If only the LORD had killed us back in Egypt,' they moaned. 'There we sat around pots filled with meat and ate all the bread we wanted. But now you have brought us into this wilderness to starve us all to death'" (Exod. 16:3 NLT). Part of our nature, even as God moves in us by his Spirit, is this odd preference for slavery. We know God wants to lead us forward, but something in us tells us we ought to stay in our hiding place, in our slavery. Right now, some of you still don't believe it. You don't believe you are God's child, and you don't believe God loves you.

Paul writes about this same idea in Galatians 4:8–9. "Formerly, when you did not know God, you were slaves to those who by nature are not gods. But now that you know God—or rather are known by God—how is it that you are turning back to those weak and miserable forces?" In essence, he's asking the Galatian Christians: "If you know what God has done—if you know you are loved—then why do you not live into it? Why do you keep trying to live according to your former condition?"

I see that so often among those I serve—those who truly have faith in Christ. They believe God loves them, but I think they remain in their own misery because they are more comfortable with what they already know. As human beings, we are naturally averse to change. We don't want to get out of our comfort zones. We don't like the unknown. So yes, God may offer us something wonderful in our identity in Christ, but we choose to live as slaves because that is the life we know. We don't know what it would mean to live as his children, but we do know slavery.

The Israelites grumbled that at least when they were slaves they had pots of food. They didn't know what the Promised

Land was, but they knew Egypt. At least in our sin, in our hiding, we know what to expect. But what kind of life is that? You've been given an inheritance to live as a child of God with all the rights and privileges of that position. Don't abdicate your place in the family of God simply because you don't know what it may mean. Don't let yourself live in the bondage of your former life. C. S. Lewis writes in *The Weight of Glory*, "We are half-hearted creatures, fooling about with drink and sex and ambition when infinite joy is offered us, like an ignorant child who wants to go on making mud pies in a slum because he cannot imagine what is meant by the offer of a holiday at the sea."[4]

I think half the time we're scared of what the holiday at the sea may be, so we go on making our mud pies. Are you kidding? Don't you see the folly of that? We need to live in our new identity created through Christ, not the former one that offers us only the empty, enslaving principles of the world. Yes, we have a nature that sometimes moves in the direction of slavery, but in those moments we need to remind ourselves of what has been offered us in Christ—a gift to which nothing can compare.

Further, if we allow ourselves to live in slavery, if we lack the courage to move toward our new identity in Christ, it will inhibit God's purpose for our lives. Do you realize that? God created you for a reason. God drew you to himself in order to accomplish a kingdom purpose far greater than your individual life. Your life gets caught up in his grander plan and vision, but if you are still stuck in your slavery, you can never live into the future he has for you.

Brennan Manning wrote of this tendency in his book *Abba's Child*: "We judge ourselves unworthy servants, and that judgment becomes a self-fulfilling prophecy. We deem ourselves too inconsiderable to be used even by a God capable of miracles with no more than mud and spit. And thus our false humility shackles an otherwise omnipotent God."[5] Uh-oh. Our inability to accept and internalize the love of God and his purpose for our life is a false idea that shackles the omnipotent God! But it does not have to be so.

Dispense with the "woe is me" self-talk. You are a child of God. You belong to the King of Kings and Lord of Lords. Royal blood courses through your veins. Stop giving in to the false judgments of our world and the false judgments you inflict on yourself. Be who you really are: God's child. Christ's disciple. God's instrument and vessel. Do you know *exactly* what that will mean for the rest of your life? Of course not. Can that be scary? Sure. But I also know it is the most rewarding, joyous, and satisfying life anyone can ever live.

I know that I don't want slavery anymore. I tried that, and that place is cold, dark, and lonely. That's the place of hiding. Come out. God is graciously pursuing you. God wants to find you. Let his love permeate your life so that you move from hiding into his wonderful, eternal presence. That's who you are—you are his. The trick is learning to live authentically out of that identity, and I'll spend the rest of this book exploring that idea. Take a few moments right now and ask God to illuminate your heart by this truth. Ask God to impress on you the person he has created you to be in Christ. Ask God to show you your true self as his child, and then read this portion of a prayer from *A Diary of Private Prayer* by John Baillie. Once you have read it, pray it from your own heart.

> O eternal God, . . . grant me this day a clear conviction of Your reality and power. Let me not seek to deaden or destroy the desire for You that disturbs my heart. Let me rather yield myself to its constraint and go where it leads me . . . and make me brave to face all the changes in my life which such vision may entail: through the grace of Christ my Savior. Amen.[6]

PART 2

Finding Our True Identity

Lisa Ling recently did a documentary segment broadcast on the Oprah Winfrey Network entitled "Pray the Gay Away?" It was an examination of how those who self-identify as gay make sense of their evangelical Christianity. She presented several radically different views, but at the end of the broadcast, she asked this question: "Were those that I observed trying to live 'straight' actually being obedient to the will of God, or were they denying who they really were?"[1] When I heard her ask it, bells and alarms sounded in my head. The question was an attempt to separate our understanding of God from our understanding of ourselves. May it never be!

It is precisely *because* we have tried to separate the two that we wind up floundering with the identity question. God is the infinite, matchless Creator of the universe. He has chosen to reveal himself to us in and through Jesus Christ. Therefore, what we believe about God shapes every other dimension of our lives. Our understanding of his nature and character will define our sense of security, our sense of self-worth, our outlook on the future, our perspective on our circumstances, our purpose in our vocation, our contentment in our finances, our endurance in our suffering, and our self-esteem through betrayal or rejection. What we believe about God affects every dimension of our lives.

Further, when we are emotionally burdened or stressed, we can often trace the root of some of that stress to something we don't believe to be true about God. For example, we can say we believe God is our provider, but our constant anxiety through the recession indicates that perhaps we actually don't believe that. I have talked with my fair share of business owners and investors who constantly wring their hands over the performance of the stock market. Sometimes I've interjected: "How do you see God providing for you in this?" Most have looked at me like I'm crazy, but a few have said, "You know what? I haven't been looking for that at all. I need to trust God in this and depend on him far more than I am." Some believed in God's provision, but most did not, and that belief was evidenced by their actions. If we find we don't believe a particular truth, then we should explore the reasons why we don't and look again at God's Word as it relates, in this case, to God's provision. For example, 1 Timothy 6:17 says that people should "put their hope in God, who richly provides us with everything for our enjoyment." Exploring those verses helps solidify our faith. We cannot disassociate our understanding of God from our understanding of ourselves. What we believe about God impacts everything. We will explore this truth further in part 2.

4

Why Do I Feel So Empty?

HOW GOD ALIGNS US
FOR THE FULLNESS OF LIFE

Two are better than one, because . . . if either of them falls
down, one can help the other up.

Ecclesiastes 4:9–10

As iron sharpens iron, so one person sharpens another.

Proverbs 27:17

He walked up the steps, crossed to the center of the platform, and turned. With each hand clutched tightly
to the sides of the pulpit, he looked up, saw the thousands
of eyes fixed on him, and wept. They, in turn, applauded.

The overwhelming emotion of that moment was born out
of the journey that had preceded it. Born in the Northeast,

William Andrews grew to 6' 9" and became a gifted basketball player, earning a scholarship to the University of Massachusetts. Injuries sidetracked his playing and practice time, so he turned to drugs and alcohol to fill the void. He finished school, got a job, entered mainstream life, and continued to use and abuse drugs.

He was, in effect, a functional addict, but that quickly ended as his addiction progressed. He lost his job. He lost his home. He lost touch with his family. He lived on the street. Working day jobs for minimum wage, his earnings immediately went to his next high. Battered by the winter's cold, he scammed a bus ticket to Orlando, Florida, only to continue in the same pattern. It was an endless cycle of begging, odd jobs, drugs, and crime, all while living under an interstate highway bridge.

Years passed. On the streets, he became known as Six Nine. He learned the system, worked the system, and continued his descent. He found that in the cold of winter, a certain doorway alcove at First Presbyterian Church provided a wave of warm air. Many nights he slept in that spot, watching the people trickle in during the wee hours of Sunday mornings to get the building ready for church. Sometimes they let him stay. Most of the time, the police made him move.

More years passed, fifteen in all, until a fateful morning when he finally understood. He bought a single hit, walked into a public bathroom in order to smoke it, but fumbled the dope out of his fingers and onto the floor. He got down on his knees and found himself looking into the filth of life— trash, condoms, needles, and bottles all gathered amid the foul smell of stale urine. As he crawled about looking for his hit, he found it atop a dried mound of vomit. He picked it up, lit it, and as he sat on the floor smoking his dope, he hit the bottom. He felt as though he might evaporate on the spot because of the yawning emptiness that was his life, his heart, and his soul. He had nothing.

Through that aching emptiness, he resolved to reconnect. He remembered the breakfast and worship service for the homeless offered by First Presbyterian Church at 6:00 on Sunday mornings. He went. A minister from Central Care Mission extended his hand, welcomed him, and told him about the gospel of Jesus Christ. In that moment, he was transformed. He quit using drugs, realigned his life, and over a period of months began to study for the ministry.

Five years later, he became a Nazarene minister serving a church in one of the poorest neighborhoods in Orlando. Two months after I became the pastor at First Presbyterian Church in the fall of 2004, he scheduled an appointment to see me. When I opened my door, I was stunned to see a 6′ 9″ black man with a wide grin standing before me. We have been friends ever since.

Our churches formed a unique relationship that has bound us together. Our communities worship together. Our leaders train together. Our men, our women, and our youth meet together. And one Sunday I invited William to preach from our pulpit—a pulpit situated within sight of the place where he had slept so many nights for so many years. Wiping away the tears, he said, "I am blessed. I am blessed." Our body, who had known of his journey, applauded.

What we saw was the joy of a man's emptiness giving way to streams of living water—streams born out of the body of Christ that had welcomed him, loved him, encouraged him, prayed for him, recognized the gifts in him, educated him, and called him to service. William had entered into the fullness of life, the abundance of life promised in John 10:10: "I have come that they may have life, and have it to the full."

Running on Empty

I am one of those people who take God at his word. If God says he came in order for us to live abundantly, then I believe that's what we are supposed to experience as his children. That does not necessarily mean financial or material abundance, but it does mean the abundance of a richly satisfying, meaningful life. Yet I often don't see that. My first book, *Vital Signs*, addressed this idea. Why is it that so many people claim to be children of God and yet do not seem to live in the fullness—the abundance—of the life he promised? Why do they seem so empty?

I'm not sure I have the entire answer for that, but at least one reason is that we have become disconnected from what makes life meaningful. We have become enamored with the idea that the main purpose of life is to increase its speed. We have no idea where we are going, but we are getting there fast. John Ortberg describes it as "hurry sickness." The pace of our life makes it tremendously difficult to connect with others or to derive any real meaning from the things we are doing. We are simply moving too fast to think about it.

Further, our interpersonal connections are increasingly virtual. They're not real. I was intrigued by a blog forwarded to me by my editor regarding the impact of Facebook on our lives. According to Tim Challies, we collectively are spending 700 billion minutes on the site each month. But it's not making us happier. It's making us miserable. He writes:

> A recent paper in *Personality and Social Psychology Bulletin* looks at a series of studies involving how people evaluate moods—their own and those of others. The study itself is not as interesting as the implications. What the study found is that people tend to underestimate how dejected other people feel and that this in turn increases a person's own sense of

unhappiness. Put otherwise, we all believe that others have better lives than we do and this makes us feel bad about ourselves.[1]

We are more technologically connected than at any time in human history, yet we are not reaping the benefits of those connections. We feel an odd sense of misery—an emptiness— that we find difficult to explain in light of the many "friends" staring back at us from the screen. How can we be empty when we have so many friends?

Not only do we have internet friends, but we now have internet worship. We no longer actually have to go somewhere for a service. Instead, we can log on to any number of live streaming services, complete with an online pastor. We never shake a hand, never look into another's eyes, never engage another human being. We are completely disconnected from community yet live with the illusion that somehow we belong. And the emptiness invades even further.

I walked into a restaurant not long ago and found a group of teenagers sitting around a table, supposedly sharing a meal together. But all nine of them were staring at cell phones while moving their thumbs over the keys. Not a single word was spoken. I could not help but wonder if they were texting each other.

We adopt the use of these technologies, connecting with people we would otherwise never communicate with, but it's all hidden behind a screen. The screen gives us an odd sense of protection and, therefore, of courage. We are slowly losing our ability to engage in honest, personal relationships. We don't know what it is to look someone in the eye and share our thoughts, our ideas, or our feelings. We can't read body language or tone on a screen, so we often misinterpret what we're reading. It seems we are losing our ability to relate honestly to others *in person*.

As our culture becomes more and more focused on self, more and more absorbed in individualism, more and more driven by technology, we are less interested in the concept of *others*. We want things our way, in our order, in our time, and at our convenience. It's all about *me*, and yet in our gut there is a nagging emptiness we can't quite put our finger on. We're running on empty.

Trying to Fill Up

Much like my friend William, we resolve to fill in our emptiness. By the grace of God, William found hope in Christ as well as a Christian community from whom he learned to live his life in a meaningful way. Many others are not as fortunate. There are plenty of groups, places, and people to connect with, but none actually fill the void.

Flash mobs are a good example. A *flash mob* is a group of people who suddenly gather in a public place, perform an unusual act focused on a particular issue, and then suddenly disperse. For instance, when Michael Jackson died, a flash mob swelled in the center of London and danced to his music. The participants didn't know each other, but they felt better by being in each other's presence. Why? They had gotten a taste of what can fill the emptiness. They had gotten a taste of what it is to share with others in the course of their human experience. They had gotten a taste of what makes life meaningful, because that is how God made us. But such a brief taste cannot satisfy. It cannot last, because just as quickly as flash mobs form, they dissipate, and people are left to fill the vacuum yet again. C. S. Lewis describes this empty chasm when he writes in *The Weight of Glory*:

> For they are not the thing itself; they are only the scent of a flower we have not found, the echo of a tune we have not heard, news from a country we have never yet visited. . . .

The sense that in this universe we are treated as strangers, the longing to be acknowledged, to meet with some response, to bridge some chasm that yawns between us and reality, is part of our inconsolable secret. . . . *Our lifelong nostalgia, our longing to be united with something in the universe from which we now feel cut off, to be on the inside of some door which we have always seen from the outside, is no mere neurotic fantasy, but the truest index of our real situation.*[2]

Our emptiness is born out of our desire to get back home, to find that place where we know we were meant to live, that place that is the very heart of God. Until that emptiness can be met in Jesus Christ, I think we will always wander. We feel cut off. We feel like outsiders. And those feelings are the truest index of our real situation. We don't want the emptiness. We want to know the answers to the questions. We want to know why we're here, what we're made for, and how we fit. We want to know who we really are, but because we have been unable to figure that out, we are left with a nagging emptiness, an unsettling feeling that we have been cut off from something, a feeling that we are somehow untethered in this vast universe.

The Root of Our Emptiness

Well, there's a reason for that. We are *relational beings*. God made us with a yearning to connect, because that hunger for relationship is what draws us to him. Thus if we continue to allow ourselves to linger in isolation while accepting counterfeit relationships, we will never know the answer to that deep longing, that inconsolable secret. We will never live out of our true selves, because we fail to understand our true identity as relational beings.

The yearning Lewis describes is not an accident. We are made as relational creatures. To understand this, we have to understand God's nature. As I said in the first few chapters, we must know God before we can know ourselves, so let me explain the origin of this truth. We worship a trinitarian God. He reveals himself to us as one God in three persons: Father, Son, and Holy Spirit. And within the Godhead, there is a relationship. German theologian Karl Barth writes, "God is the One who seeks and finds relationship. He is Himself, and therefore to everything outside Himself, relationship, the basis and prototype of all relationship."[3] There is a wonderful text in Genesis 1 that provides us a glimpse of this truth. As God is working through the steps of creation, he says, "Let us make mankind in our image, in our likeness." Who is God talking to? No one else is around, yet he says, "Let us . . ." (Gen. 1:26).

It is the first revelation of God as trinitarian. God is related within himself as Father, Son, and Holy Spirit. As hard as that is for us to wrap our finite brains around, it is true. God, within his nature, is a relational being. We were made in his likeness; therefore, we are relational beings as well. How can we be anything else? From the foundations of the world, God essentially said, "I want you to be like me. I want you to be in relationship with each other as a reflection of my nature and your ultimate relationship with me." Every human relationship we have is merely a placeholder for the perfection of our fulfilled relationship with God in the beauty of eternity. One is a faint taste of the other.

So between now and the ultimate fulfillment of our relationship with God in eternity, we are in relationship with each other. God calls us to be together. Paul describes it well in 1 Corinthians 12:13: "For we were all baptized by one Spirit so as to form one body—whether Jews or Gentiles, slave or free—and we were all given the one Spirit to drink." When we come to know God through Christ, he immediately plants us in a body. He says, in effect, "You are a part of my family, a family that joins you with many brothers and sisters. Regardless of what they are like or where they are from, you are bound together through me, so be in relationship with each other." That reality is what transformed the life of my friend William. Not only did he find Christ, but he was placed by Christ into a body that functioned as it was supposed to.

This is echoed in Scripture over and over again. God never calls us into isolation but always into community. Acts 2 is a wonderful reminder of this as the early Christian church began to grow. The word *together* is mentioned numerous times. God does not reveal his saving grace in Christ and then tell us to go be alone. No! He says go and live in relationship, because when those relationships are grounded in God, they become the strength and sustenance of our lives until our relationship with him can be fulfilled eternally.

And guess what? We need each other. I love the text in 1 Kings 19:7 when Elijah is fleeing for his life from Jezebel. He is defeated, alone, and discouraged. He even asks God to end his life. But an angel appears and says, "Get up and eat, for the journey is too much for you." Elijah was trying to do it by himself at that point, but God says, "Look, you can't do it. The journey of life is too much to handle alone." And so it is. Life is hard. It's challenging. It's painful. Knowing this, God created us to do it together. God created us to be part of a larger community, a community in which we can be in relationship with others through our relationship with Christ.

While that sounds relatively simple, it is enormously challenging in practice. Almost from birth we are taught to be independent, self-sufficient, and strong. We are taught that needing someone else is a sign of weakness. If you watch television long enough, you will hear the message of our time: *You are your own god. It lies within yourself to meet your needs and make yourself happy.* It's a lie, yet we desperately try to live out of that identity. We keep telling ourselves, "I am a strong person. I can handle this. I don't need anyone else."

I call it my "Simon and Garfunkel identity": "I am a rock. I am an island." I'm not going to feel any pain, and I'm never going to cry, because nothing can reach me or touch me. I am a strong, self-sufficient person. My goodness, how we human beings love to sing that song! Yet honestly, what kind of life is that? We may think it's true for a time, but eventually we'll discover we cannot do it alone. Eventually we'll discover our true identity as relational beings. It is not what we've been taught, so we have to learn to be in relationship with God and others.

The Beauty of the Church

It is for this reason that I love the church. The church of Jesus Christ, with all its many iterations and expressions, is the earthly community of the family of God. In individual churches all over the world, God allows us the privilege of living out our lives together. Jesus Christ is the incarnation of God. By the presence of the Holy Spirit, the church is the evidence of that ongoing incarnation. The church becomes the presence of Jesus to the world. It is no mistake that the church is called the body of Christ (Eph. 5:29–30). We are his earthly, living body. Now let's try to understand what that means.

Paul said in 1 Corinthians 12 that the church is a "body." The physical image of a body is obviously one that is multi-faceted, but primarily what Paul creates is an image of a unified whole. The body is one entity—one unit—and all of us who profess faith are a part of it. We are not disconnected; we are connected. We are not isolated; we are joined. Here's the good news: God has made the church his earthly body, his earthly community, and we are all part of it. You're not out; you're in. You're not excluded; you're included. God's desire for us is that we never live apart. We are always a part of something, and our part of that something is significant. God, revealed to us as Father, Son, and Holy Spirit, is a relational being—one God in three persons. So as his earthly body, we too are related to each other and part of a unified whole.

This does not mean the community will function perfectly or purely. We're sort of like the folks you find when you go to those big family reunions. You show up at the family cookout, take a look at some of your relatives, and think, *Wow, this must be the shallow end of the gene pool. I'm not even sure I like these people.* Remember, there are people thinking the same thing about you. It's true of the church as well. I have heard it said, "The church would be a great place if it weren't for the people." We're just people—sinful, fallen, frail people. That's why we're in church, right? We need a Savior.

In his book *Love One Another,* Gerald Sittser writes, "When the church is functioning at her best, there is simply no community on earth that can rival it. But when the church is functioning at her worst, there is no community on earth that can do as much damage."[4] It's true. Churches can certainly make a mess of things. We, as parts of the church, will never be perfect, but there is something in us that falsely assumes the church will never make a mistake or let us down. But knowing what we know, how could that be? If you expect perfection, then yes, you will always be disappointed by the church. You will always be let down.

But if you understand the church as the divinely created body of Christ, broken and yet filled by his Spirit, then you will see everything through a different lens. You will see the beauty and wonder of being connected to the bride, his church. Paul writes, "Christ loved the church and gave himself up for her . . . to present her to himself as a radiant church, without stain or wrinkle or any other blemish, but holy and blameless" (Eph. 5:25, 27). That's God's vision of his church. That's the community we have been called to be part of, and we need to reclaim that vision.

It makes me sad when I hear people rail against the "institutional" church. People look at what is happening—theological controversies, moral failures, questionable spending, bureaucratically slow processes—and they say, "I don't want to be a part of that. I am going to do it my way. I'm a believer, but I don't want to be a part of the institutional church." That is a complete contradiction, because in the process they are isolating themselves. That's like being an elbow and saying, "Look at how inefficient this body is—the heart and lungs aren't too good—there's too much flab around the middle—so I'm going to stay over here by myself." What good does this do? An elbow apart from the body is of no use whatsoever.

The church is to be God's earthly body, his earthly community. No matter the errors the church has made or the problems the church has caused, we are a part of it and we need to connect deeply into her so that our body reflects to the world the love, grace, and goodness of God. While Christ's church must function with institutional qualities in order to execute her mission, she is not defined by those qualities. She is who God has made her to be: his divinely created bride for which he gave his life. That's what we connect to. That's where we find relationship. That's where we learn to live out of our true identity.

So ask yourself:

Am I living in quiet isolation apart from a church because I have been wounded or hurt before?

Am I living in isolation because a church body made a decision I did not like?

Am I living apart because I don't trust institutions?

If you are disconnected from the church for any reason, reconnect. Challenge yourself to visit some new churches or perhaps one you have not been to in a while. You'll never find a perfect body, so stop looking for it. Find a biblical, Christ-centered church, and then invest in it. Reach out. Get involved. Sink down some roots. Commit. Don't be a pew sitter. Serve. Engage. That's when you build relationships. That's when you connect. When you connect with a church community, you move against cultural isolation and you answer that internal longing. You start living as you were meant to live.

The Impact of Community

The way in which the church is a community has ramifications not only for us but also for the wider community. This is an essential part of our witness to the world. That's part of why God brings us together, why we are baptized into one body. Randy Frazee writes in his book *The Connecting Church*, "In a culture of individualism, when do non-Christians get to see other Christians loving each other in such a way that it compels them to run to Jesus Christ? The church has often mirrored the culture by making Christianity an individual sport."[5] We have, haven't we? We have put so much emphasis on Bible studies and other ministries that cater to our spiritual growth that we have inadvertently fostered a spiritual individualism that is decidedly not God's plan. We start to adopt the idea that our faith is about us. We think God is in heaven to meet our needs. No. God created us to be part of his church in order to advance his kingdom, period. Therefore if we withdraw from the body of Christ and isolate ourselves from community, we miss the opportunity to live out of our true identity.

Andy Stanley, in his book *Christian Community*, quotes the late Francis Schaeffer: "Our relationship with each other is the criterion the world uses to judge whether our message is truthful—Christian community is the final apologetic"[6] (the final way in which we defend and demonstrate what it is we believe). I wonder if a non-Christian came and looked at the community of your church or my church, would our community—the way we are together, the way we love each other and speak about each other and give to one another and worship with each other—would this cause that person to run *to* Jesus Christ or away from him?

Finding Some Help

I must admit this whole idea of togetherness can sound daunting. Honestly, it's much easier to stay isolated and disconnected, because then nothing is required of us. We don't have to invest in others or care for others or do anything that makes us uncomfortable. We also avoid the possibility of being hurt by never allowing ourselves to be emotionally close to others. And by living in isolation, we also keep others from speaking honestly into our lives. We never have to change or grow, because we have no relational accountability. Even so, aren't those also the very things that make life rich and satisfying?

Living in relationship with others is hard, and no doubt, we need help. Thankfully, we can receive help from the Holy Spirit and from other believers. The power of the Spirit of God helps us move from an inward-looking life to an outward-looking one in which we are connected to his body. When we trust in Jesus Christ by faith, the Holy Spirit comes to live in us to guide and illuminate the things of God in Christ (John 16:13–14). As that happens, we want the things of God more and we want the world less. Consequently, the things of this world recede, including the things that typically separate us. Our unity in Christ unites us in a far more powerful way than any earthly barrier can divide us.

Gerald Sittser writes in *Love One Another*:

> The more genuine and the deeper our community becomes, the more everything else between us will recede, the more clearly and purely will Jesus Christ and His work become the one and only thing that is vital between us. We have one another only through Christ, but through Christ we have one another—for all eternity.[7]

How do we ever experience the community that God desires for us? It's possible because the Spirit of Jesus lives in each of us and empowers us to do things and be people that we never thought we could be. Why do you think the church still exists today, given all her mistakes and blunders over the years? How do you think a group of twelve people with relatively no education led a religious movement that overtook the entire planet? They had help. They had the power of the Holy Spirit.

Our other source of help is the other members of the body. Galatians 6:2 reminds us, "Bear . . . one another's burdens" (KJV). Proverbs 27:17 calls us to "sharpen" each other. We have an important role to play frequently in each other's lives—accountability. We are not free, independent agents answering to no one. We are the children of God who are called to live lives of obedience and faithfulness as we love God and love others. Unfortunately, a problem rises out of our sinful nature. Our natural inclination is to pursue our own desires instead of God's. I don't like it, but I know I lean in that direction. So I need others in the body to hold me accountable to my true nature in Christ and not my old, sinful one. I want to live for real, but I also know myself well enough to know that if left to my own devices, I will fail miserably. I will live out of my counterfeit, worldly self.

So how does this play out? I believe we need others in our lives to whom we grant permission to get up in our business and ask us hard questions. I need others who will not leave me alone, who will not allow me to become isolated, but who will draw me into the presence of God and help me be the person he has made me to be. This has been a discipline I have followed since college. No matter where I live or what church I am called to, I always ask the Lord to provide a group of men who will love me enough to tell me the hard things. While they have been easier to find at some times than at others, God has always been faithful to provide them.

Let me give you an example: I was in a group with a dear friend who struggled with pornography when he traveled. He shared his failures in this area and asked that we hold him accountable. So for months afterward, whenever he traveled, one of us called him each night to ask how he was doing. The knowledge that he would have to answer to us helped him find the strength to live out of his true nature in Christ, not the sinful nature that desires the things of this world.

That said, accountability works only insofar as you are willing to use it. You can be in a Bible study or an account- ability group, but if you never share your true struggles or if you lie about your true progress, then the group never has the opportunity to help you. You'll be on the same island you were before, and make no mistake, you'll fall. We all know countless examples of personal friends and public figures who had the opportunity for accountability but didn't use it. They didn't reveal their temptations or struggles to trusted friends, and therefore they stumbled in their journey. We need accountability in our lives, and when we have it, we need to use it. We have to trust it.

You need this, so go find it. Pray. Examine the current relationships in your life. Find two or three others of the same gender and agree to meet regularly—at least twice per month. Start with a shared understanding of trust and confidentiality. Then honestly share your stories. Perhaps begin with an overnight retreat so you have uninterrupted time to do this. Then bring focus to your conversations by sharing your current circumstances. What problems are you facing? What temptations are you struggling with? Where do you need to deepen your walk with the Lord? Pray for each other. Read Scripture together. Find books you can read together that address the issues discussed. Get to know each other's families. Tell your spouse about it. And of course, use it. Get up in the face of your friends when they need it. And when they do the same for you, give thanks that God has given you friends to keep you from isolation and to help you walk the journey. It's too much for you, so find some others who will do it with you.

In our church, one of my favorite examples comes from our jail ministry. We have a group of women who weekly go into our county jail to minister to incarcerated women. What's amazing is how these two totally different groups of women connect. Sitting in the chapel together, they look nothing alike, and yet they bond with each other and encourage each other because of one thing: the unity they have in Christ. That is the power of community. It is the power of the Spirit of God at work through broken, humbled people.

That's who you are. That is your true identity. God is related within his nature, and he made you in his image, so you are a relational being. You need others. Therefore, do all you can to move out of the isolation of your life and into relationship with others, especially through the community of faith that is the church of Jesus Christ.

If you are already in a church, then examine that community in order to deepen it. As you look at your church, do you see a connected body of believers who are growing in faith as well as bearing fruitful ministry in the world? Or do you see a group of individuals who attend in order to feel better about themselves but who do not connect to the larger kingdom purpose of the body? Going back to Mark 3, Jesus called the disciples that they "might be with him and that he might send them out" (v. 14). Christian community exists for a twofold purpose: (1) to be nurtured in the context of a common faith, and (2) to be sent out with others to change the world for God's kingdom. It is the antidote to emptiness.

So examine your life. Are you feeling the aching emptiness born out of the patterns of our modern world, or have you been filled by the love of God and connected into a community that aligns your life for purposeful, kingdom living? William Andrews at one time was an empty man. Today that emptiness has been replaced because of his faith in Christ and the way Christ has connected him into his larger family, a family united for Christ's glory. Your identity is as a relational being. Don't let your emptiness get you down. Get up. Look around. Open yourself to a relationship with Jesus. Connect with a church. Unite with others for his glory, and you'll soon discover your empty days are over!

5

Does My Life Make a Difference?

HOW GOD EMPOWERS US
TO CHANGE HIS WORLD

I am God, and there is no other; I am God, and there is none
like me. . . . I say, "My purpose will stand, and I will do all
that I please."

Isaiah 46:9–10

The King and Trufflehunter and Doctor Cornelius were expecting—well, if you see what I mean, help. To put it another
way, I think they'd been imagining you as great warriors. As
it is—we're awfully fond of children . . . but I'm sure you
understand.

Trumpkin to the children in Prince Caspian by C. S. Lewis

Everyone does dumb, foolish, unwise, ridiculous things
at some time in his or her life. Here's a story from my
personal file.

In the summer of 2007, I was invited to Wycliffe Hall Seminary, Oxford, for several days of preaching and teaching with their students. I was thrilled at the prospect, and because our family had never been to Europe, we decided to make a family trip out of it. With the help of some knowledgeable friends in Orlando, we planned for several days in Oxford and several days in London and Paris. Needless to say, it was a thrilling experience made all the more special by having my entire family with me.

The most memorable moment of our trip, however, was not our time at Oxford, though we loved every minute of that. The most memorable moment was the result of something very foolish I did while in Paris. On one of our days in that great city, we decided to visit the Louvre. If you have never been to this magnificent museum, it is hard to describe its magnitude. It is enormous. Cavernous. You couldn't possibly see it in a month, let alone a day, but that was all the time we had, so we made the attempt. To be clear, I am not exactly an arts aficionado. I'm generally not one who visits museums for fun, so I tend to run out of energy quickly when visiting such places. My max is about three hours. So at the Louvre I saw the things I wanted to see: the Mona Lisa, a few paintings by Rembrandt—you know—the biggies. It was great. I thoroughly enjoyed seeing them, but by late afternoon, I was done.

Thankfully, my children were done too. John David was fifteen at the time, Alex was fourteen, and Kaylee was twelve. I think their appreciation for the art was even less than mine! So I decided it was time for the kids and me to head back to the hotel. My wife, Leigh, wanted to keep looking, so we left her and her mother at the museum and took off to get a cab. When we got to the cabstand, it started to rain, but there were no cabs. After about fifteen minutes, a little cab—an Audi no less—pulled up. We were all soaked, so we opened the door and started to pile in. As we did, the cabdriver rudely blurted, "No. Not four. Three." I thought, *What is he talking about?* Obviously he was not an American, and I'm quite sure he wasn't French either, but two things were certain: he didn't want to take four of us, and he didn't seem to like me.

In fact, there were a number of people in France who didn't seem to like me, but that's another matter. There was ample room in the car, but in spite of my protests, he kept repeating, "Not four. Three." It was at that point, standing in my wet clothes, that I made a strategic error. My thought was to get the kids out of the rain, so I took out my wallet, gave twenty Euros to John David, and said, "You guys go ahead. I'll meet you back at the hotel." As the cab pulled away, I knew immediately that I had made a huge mistake. It suddenly occurred to me that I had just put my three very American children in a cab with a driver who did not like me in a foreign city that my children knew nothing about. I thought, *I'll never see my kids again. Leigh is going to kill me.*

Squelching my rising panic, I flagged down another cab, and we took off. But as we approached Concord Plaza, an enormous roundabout encircled by a sea of cars, I realized I had given John David my last twenty Euros. I had no money. So I had to weigh an ethical dilemma: Do I tell the cabdriver now or when we arrive? My integrity got the best of me and I held up my empty wallet and said, "No Euros."

With that, in a driving rain in the middle of Concord Plaza, the cabdriver angrily kicked me out of his cab. Somehow I managed to dodge traffic and get out of the circle without getting killed, much to the cabdriver's disappointment. And then I really did panic. I had no other options, so I started running.

Frantic, I ran in my leather shoes for about twenty minutes— I'm guessing about two miles—all the way back to the hotel.

Looking like a drowned rat, I reached the lobby of our hotel and rushed for the house phone. The desk clerk gave me one of those looks that said, "You dumb American," but I found the phone anyway—called their room—and John David answered, saying, "Dad, where have you been? We've been back here for thirty minutes. We're hungry." Gratefully, I had avoided the headline in Orlando that would have read, "Pastor Loses Children in Paris; Wife Shoots Him." I also noticed that over the last few days of our trip, Leigh didn't leave me alone with our children—ever. It was not my best moment in fathering.

I have never felt as helpless or powerless as I did in those twenty minutes running back to the hotel. I had control over nothing. As I have reflected on that experience, especially the intensity of those feelings, I think it may be an effective image for how many of us feel today. When we consider the current societal circumstances and the intense pressures people are experiencing in their personal lives, those feelings of powerlessness and panic are often just below the surface, if not already on it.

We learn to mask the panic, but it's there. As I write:

- our country continues to muddle through a devastating recession
- home foreclosures are at an all-time high
- the Middle East is a boiling cauldron of change and reform in the wake of Egypt's overthrow of Hosni Mubarak and protests in Syria
- Iran and North Korea threaten to develop long-range nuclear weapons
- half the world's population is malnourished or dying from nutrition-related issues
- unexpected natural disasters like the devastating earthquake and tsunami in Japan and the earthquake and

hurricane that struck Haiti have cost billions of dollars
and caused a staggering loss of life

It's no wonder we have a population of people who are scared
and anxious about their future. And those are just the outside issues.

Individually, people face constant pressure in regard to
health, marriage, children, work, and finances. No matter
how hard we try, we feel powerless to make a difference in
any of it. We cannot change the test results. We cannot erase
the wounds in our marriage. We cannot make our children
love us. We cannot make the financial numbers work. The
resulting anxiety creates a lot of people who are frantically
running like I did in Paris, overwhelmed with a feeling that
our lives really don't matter in the face of such daunting
challenges. We feel powerless.

Naturally, when we lose our sense of power, we start looking desperately for answers, but the ones we find leave us
empty. Doubts swell and the panic we have suppressed rises
in the absence of a truth on which we know we can stand. As
we try to make sense of all the issues and all the competing
ideologies that promise solutions, we are left like rain-soaked
tourists, frantically running, searching for help, overwhelmed
by our inability to change our lives or our world.

The result, of course, is a weakened sense of who we are.
Our identity becomes filled by a hopeless sense of determin-
ism. We're on a path, and there's nothing we can do about
it. It's depressing. And because we lack the power to effect
change in our world, we quit trying. Far from grasping any
concept that "I can do all things through Christ who strength-
ens me" (Phil. 4:13 NKJV), we fold into a weakened state,
living a life far less than the one God intended. If that's the
case, where's the answer? Where do we find hope?

Our hope is found when we understand the true nature of God, and so our true identity as his children. God is very much alive, and he is omnipotent. Not only does he have power, but he is all-powerful. There is none like him, and our confidence and our peace soar when we consider what effect that omnipotence could have in our lives and in our world.

The Power of Remembering

If you find yourself feeling weak or lacking power, Isaiah 46 is a good place to turn to plug back into the Power Source. The people of Israel are confronting some of the same issues we are. In spite of God's faithfulness to Israel for generations, the Israelites have turned from the Lord, rebelled, and followed the idols and false gods of Babylon. The result is exile and powerlessness. The search for answers leads the Israelites to follow the cultural idols of the time and listen to everyone but God. That's not too far from what we're doing right now. Out of control and powerless, we turn to the cultural idols of our time in order to numb the pain and quell the panic. We are so desperate for an answer that works, we'll try just about anything. We bow at the altar of materialism; we bow at the altar of secularism; we bow at the altar of standardless inclusivity; we bow at the altars of pleasure, substance abuse, and success; and the list goes on. We believe these things will make us more powerful, at least until the façade is shattered and we find ourselves looking for yet another altar.

It is here, into this confused time in Israel, that God speaks. In effect, he says, "You have forgotten who I am. You have forgotten my nature. How can those idols you worship have any power when you have to carry them? It is I who carry you!" In Isaiah 46:8–9, he twice tells them, "Remember." As we struggle to live in such a time as this, the power of our memory is the tool God uses to encourage and strengthen us.

Sadly, I have learned this the hard way recently. We all go through seasons in our lives when things are busy, complicated, stressful—you know the feeling. The fall of 2010 was that way for me, and my answer was to burn my candle at both ends trying to do everything. I was depending on my own personal strength and resolve, and gradually I grew distant from the Lord. As challenging events occurred, I could not fight off strong feelings of personal weakness and exhaustion. I was whipped, and as much as I wished for his help, God seemed distant and uninvolved.

I was about at my breaking point when our church held its annual leadership weekend led by Fil Anderson. Fil is a marvelous, humble, Christ-following leader whom God used to bring me back from the brink. Fil said we all struggle with "spiritual amnesia." I love that term. He said the reason we often feel helpless and powerless in who we are is because we have largely forgotten who God is. We have forgotten the powerful nature of the one who fills our lives. It was a simple yet profound *aha* moment for me.

The next day, I got my old journals out and began reading. I went back to the Scriptures, especially the Old Testament, and lingered in all that God had done. Wow. Suddenly my realization of God's power at work throughout my past was rekindled, and my identity felt reborn as a child of the King. In fact, my word for this year has been *remember*. Whenever I get in a place where I feel overwhelmed or powerless, I check my spirit and I remember. I remember whom I worship. I remember who put the stars in the sky. I remember the cross. I remember who fills me, and I yield whatever I'm facing to him and trust in his power within me to work it out. I have not mastered it, but I am learning how to fight my spiritual amnesia.

Creator and Redeemer

When we reflect on God's power, we would do well to remember two things that Isaiah 46 illuminates. First, the power of our God is unmatched, and often that power is revealed by the creation around us. Put simply, there are no other gods. In Isaiah 46:9 he says, "Remember . . . I am God, and there is no other; I am God, and there is none like me." In that moment, he calls on the name he gave to Moses in Exodus 3. He tells them to remember "*I am*." God is essentially saying, "Remember that I am the God who has always been and will always be. I am. I make known the end from the beginning. Remember." God is the one who has set all things in motion. God is our Creator. Psalm 19:1 tells us, "The heavens declare the glory of God." Even as the atheists tell us there is no God, we would do well to consider the evidence revealed by the heavens around us.

Second, not only is God all-powerful in respect to the universe, but he is also all-powerful in regard to salvation. God is our Redeemer. He says in Isaiah 46:12–13, "Listen to me, you stubborn-hearted, you who are now far from my righteousness. I am bringing my righteousness near, it is not far away; and my salvation will not be delayed." That may well be the best description of the human heart in all of Scripture. We are stubborn-hearted, and we are blind to how that stubborn nature drives us further and further away from the very thing we're trying to find. We all want to find life, but we keep wandering in the wrong places. We are the prodigal son, living according to our own desires. We rationalize to ourselves, "I'll figure this out. I'll make it work. I can do it." And with each choice, we keep getting further and further away. So what does God do? He moves toward us. He says, "I'll bring my righteousness to you." The implication is: *You can't get to me. You're too stubborn. So*

I'll come to you. God uses his power for a purpose; he uses it to save. It is his nature.

Clark Kent in a Phone Booth

The result of God's power moving toward us in Christ, creating us, and redeeming us is mind-blowing. When we yield to the power of God's love and redemption, we become *empowered* people. His power lives in us, and his empowering Spirit defines our true identity. We are not powerless. We are powerful, not in our own strength, but in his. He says in Isaiah 46:10, "My purpose will stand, and I will do all that I please." Then in verse 13, "I will grant salvation to Zion, my splendor to Israel." How did the nature of God become manifest in the world? He used Israel. Israel repented, returned from exile, reclaimed the homeland, and again became the vessel through which God reveals himself to the world.

Here's the verse I love from that same narrative, just a few chapters earlier: "Do not be afraid, you worm Jacob, little Israel, . . . for I myself will help you. . . . I will make you into a threshing sledge, new and sharp, with many teeth. You will thresh the mountains and crush them" (Isa. 41:14–15). The most powerful tool of that time was a threshing sledge. It was a huge, heavy, flat piece of iron with metal teeth underneath it. It was used to churn up ground for planting or clear ground to make room for paths, homes, or planting fields.

God first called Israel weak and wormy. Not a bad description for how we feel sometimes—powerless. But when God comes and enters Israel, it's like Clark Kent going into a phone booth. He goes in as a normal, nerdy man and comes out with powers untold. Israel goes in wormy and weak and then emerges in the power of God as the most powerful instrument in the world!

What God did in Israel—transforming a weak, powerless nation into a powerful instrument in his hand—is exactly what he can do in our lives. No matter the nature of our rebellion or the extent of our current exile, no matter the depth of our fear or anxiety, he wants his power to be made manifest in us. The problem we have with that is we think it means we are going to be able to function like a superhero. Not so.

Let me explain. I was driving some teenage guys on my son's basketball team to a tournament last summer, and they had the most hilarious conversation regarding the relative power of each superhero, trying to decide which was the greatest. These juniors and seniors in high school compared the virtues of Superman, Batman, Aquaman, Spiderman, and the Hulk and then tried to work through logically which one was superior. You see, we love that kind of power. We want to wave a wand and have God's power take away our pain, heal our diseases, and help us leap tall buildings in a single bound. When it doesn't happen, we think God's power is not real. We need to remember, however, that those things are not what God promised.

Practical Power Places

In *Discover God*,[1] Bill Bright reminds us of five distinct areas in which the power of God is manifest in our lives. These are places in our lives where we can again reclaim our true identity as a person filled by the power of God.

1. *You have the power to conquer evil forces.* Luke 10:19 reminds us that God has given us power over the enemy and he cannot injure us. You can defeat evil where you find it. That's why one of my favorite shows, while it ran, was *Buffy the Vampire Slayer*. I heard someone say the show had gospel implications, so I tuned in. I was amazed. She was this cute

little blonde who was worried about her nails and the grade she was going to make in algebra. She looked like she had no power at all. But who was she really? She was the vampire slayer. She had the power to vanquish evil. People around her struggled to do it, but she whipped the vampires every time. She didn't look very powerful, but she was. That's who we are. We don't look like much, but we're Buffy. We have the power of God within us. That's our true identity. Live into it. By the Holy Spirit alive and at work in you, you can conquer evil where you find it in your life.

2. *You have the power to live a holy life that honors God.* Second Peter 1:3 says, "His divine power has given us everything we need for a godly life." We may not always make the right choices because of that stubborn nature in us, but we need to remember that we have the *power* to make the right choice. We can do it because we live in relationship with a powerful God. Don't sell yourself short. Don't think you are beaten. Too often our besetting sins are used by the enemy to discourage and weaken us. No! Recognize the power you have to live a godly life. Create a plan to defeat what currently tempts you. Like any general going into battle, you need a plan. You don't go up against an experienced enemy without knowing what you're going to do. You have the greatest, most powerful army on your side, so use it. Call on the body of Christ. Build accountability into your life. Enlist prayer partners. Change your self-talk by memorizing Scripture. These are all powerful tools at your disposal. Use them as you endeavor to live as a disciple of Christ.

3. *You have power in your weakness.* In 2 Corinthians 12:9, God reminds us, "My grace is sufficient for you, for my power is made perfect in weakness." When you can't, he can—and he does. Not with the waving of a magic wand that makes it all go away, but with the faithful presence of his Spirit reminding

us that he has already conquered all we suffer and that our suffering allows us to identify more and more with his suffering and the extent of his love for us. God uses our weak moments redemptively in our lives, but too often we want to pray ourselves out of those moments. This is where our false superhero assumptions often get the best of us. When we feel weak, we want to jump into a phone booth and become someone else in order to avoid any pain or hardship. Not so with God. Instead, he says he will be with us. We need not flee. Our power is in his presence. So often in life when we encounter loss or hardships that threaten to break us, what allows us to carry on? The presence of others. Their presence seems to transfer their strength to us, allowing us to go on. So it is in Christ. He comes to be with us and assures us he will never leave.

4. *You have power to proclaim the gospel, to tell people the Good News of God's redeeming love in Christ.* You have the power to share something that can transform another's life. That's what I love about my job. I am in the Good News business. With all due respect to my friends in the news media, I would so much rather have my job than theirs. They have to tell people bad news every day. It would stink if you had to be the guy every night who said, "The price of oil reached another new high today" or "Breaking news on a double murder downtown." I get to share the Good News, and in the process, there is the potential that another's life will be transformed. Plus, when I communicate the hope of the gospel, my perspective changes. I can get swallowed up by the issues in our church, but when I sit down to study Scripture and prepare my sermons, the Good News always changes my heart. Once again, I remember. I have God's power. You have God's power. You have the power to let the Good News flow in you and through you, and as you share it, you are empowered by the very truth you proclaim.

5. *You have the power to fulfill God's plan for you.* God never calls you to do something that he does not also equip you for. Your task is obedience. Your task is to show up. Your task is to walk through the doors he opens. You have the power of God in you to do what he wants you to do. When I was in my early twenties and suffering from debilitating panic attacks, I thought there was no way I could ever be a pastor. Yet my resolve was to keep walking through any door God opened, trusting he would give me the power to do what had to be done on that day. And he always did. He never failed, nor will he. The challenge is to believe in his power enough to act on it and live out his plan for your life. Go ahead. You have the power. Act on what God is calling you to do.

Child Warriors

In the second book of C. S. Lewis's Chronicles of Narnia series, he tells the story of Prince Caspian. Peter, Susan, Edmund, and Lucy are summoned back to Narnia by Susan's horn, which had been left there as a means of summoning help for the Narnians. When they arrive, Narnia is in disarray. Massive trouble awaits. The four children stand before Trumpkin, the dwarf, ready for their instructions. Trumpkin says, "I suppose I'd better go back to King Caspian and tell him no help has come." Susan says, "No help? But [the horn] *has* worked—don't you see who we are?" To which Trumpkin replies, "The King and Trufflehunter and Doctor Cornelius were expecting—well, if you see what I mean, help. To put it another way, I think they'd been imagining you as great warriors. As it is—we're awfully fond of children and all that, but just at the moment, in the middle of a war—but I'm sure you understand."[2]

The Narnians call for help, but when only weak-looking children arrive, they assume their doom is sealed. Not so. The weak-looking children are actually mighty warriors, and Lewis reminds us all of that truth. The story ends with the children winning the day because they fight in the power of the mighty Lion, Aslan, the Christ-figure of Lewis's story. And so it is with us.

We are children, no doubt. We live in the cold reality of our own helplessness. We live in search of a power that works. We find that power when we go back to—when we remember— the true nature of our God and his power to create, save, and redeem. Children? Yes. But also those filled by his power to live as his victorious servants in this world. That's who God is—and thus we are children of the King. May our true identity be found as we live out of that power.

6

Why Am I Alone?

HOW GOD'S PRESENCE ANSWERS
OUR YEARNING TO CONNECT

> Where can I go from your Spirit?
>   Where can I flee from your presence? . . .
> Even the darkness will not be dark to you;
>   the night will shine like the day,
>   for darkness is as light to you.
>
> Psalm 139:7, 12

> Friendship needs no words—it is solitude delivered from the anguish of loneliness.
>
> Dag Hammarskjold

In the summer of 2008, a rather interesting scene unfolded early one morning in New York City. At about four in the morning on Wednesday, July 9, a line started to form.

It began at the Manhattan Center, a concert venue on 34th Street. Starting at the stage, it went down the center aisle, then back and down the side aisle, then out a door, into the lobby, up the stairs and into the balcony, then back down again and out the door onto the street. When you got in line, you were given a numbered token as a placeholder. That was just the line to be in the line.

Most waited seven hours or more to receive what they had come for. Do you suppose it was a line for the latest Apple product? Was it a line for the latest New York play or show? Was it a line to get a book or an autograph from a great public figure? No, it was none of those things. It was a line for hugs. That's right, hugs. The person doing the hugging was a fifty-four-year-old Hindu woman named Mata Amritanandamayi, also known to her followers as Amma, or mother.

She has been traveling around the world for the past eighteen years, attracting crowds just like that summer morning in New York. It is estimated that she has hugged 27 million people in her lifetime. When a person approaches her for a hug, Amma grasps him or her with one arm first, then two, and pulls the person toward her. Each one lasts about thirty seconds, and the person gets a Hershey's chocolate kiss when he or she leaves. There are 150 unpaid volunteers who work with Amma just so they can be near her, so they can be hugged on a regular basis. One woman said, "It feels like sunshine or moonlight shining on me." Another said, "I feel the best part of humankind." Amma spent three days at the Manhattan Center, hugging almost nonstop until the last of more than eight thousand people had been hugged.[1]

When I first saw the story, I thought, *What a phenomenal waste of time. If you need a hug, come on down to my office—there's no line!* In all honesty, I thought it was oddly sad. The entire event speaks to the state of our culture and the deep, deep yearning we have to be embraced—to be loved—to feel that somehow, even for just thirty seconds, we are not alone. Every day thousands upon thousands of people live out their lives with one dominant reality: they are alone.

Being alone, for many of us, is one of our greatest fears. It's why so many horror movies depict characters alone in a house being stalked by monsters or masked men wielding chain saws. They prey upon our deep-seated fear of being alone. It's why we are drawn to movies like *Cast Away*. We think, *What would that be like? Could I survive on a deserted island, alone, for four years?* We relate to Tom Hanks's character when he goes slightly insane in his loneliness and begins a relationship with a volleyball he appropriately names Wilson. I once mentioned this scene in a sermon, and the next week someone sent me my own "Wilson." He now sits on my desk, and I must admit, there are times when he comes in handy.

To be sure, some experiences we have in life make this feeling all the more acute. Death is the most obvious one. A woman who had recently lost her father said to me, "With my mother already gone, it feels strange, like I am suddenly all alone." Losing those we love can often leave us with an aching sense of loneliness, but there are other moments that can cause that feeling as well: Moving. Changing jobs. Ending a relationship. Being betrayed in a relationship. Regardless, we yearn for the presence of another, and whether we know it or not, that yearning is for the presence of God.

The problem, of course, is that we often don't feel God's presence. He's not present in the way we want him to be present. The constant reminders from pastors like me that "God is with you always" seem almost disingenuous in light of real-life circumstances. Our hearts cry out, "Well, if God is here, then why don't I feel him?" We know what Joshua 1:9 says: "Be strong and courageous. . . . For the LORD your God will be with you wherever you go." We want that to be true, and yet if we're honest, there are moments when it feels as though he's not there. And there are seasons when it feels as though God is millions of miles away from us. We feel like many Hindus who ritually go around tapping on trees, saying, "Are you in there? Are you in there?" They are hoping to find the presence of one of the gods they worship—somewhere—anywhere.

In addition, as we yearn for God's presence, we hear the cultural skeptics telling us he's not real and thus certainly not present. We hear people like Christopher Hitchens, Samuel Harris, and Richard Dawkins aggressively contend that there is no God, thus his spiritual presence is merely a feeling fabricated by a needy human mind. It is a condescending argument with nothing behind it, but it still pricks our confidence to be told we're stupid. So as we try to find the presence of God, these ideas cloud our mind and make us doubt whether we can really be in the presence of God.

Look Who's Here

Is God really with us? Are we really alone in this world after all? No, we are not alone, and that answer is expressed quite powerfully in one of David's psalms. Psalm 139 is one of the most well-read and oft-quoted passages in the Old Testament, primarily because it provides the truth we so deeply long to hear. It is a soaring description of who God is in his *omnipresence*—his ability to be everywhere, always, in the fullness of his being.

Through beautiful Hebrew poetry, David paints a picture of God's presence in every direction—north, south, east, and west. In verses 8–10 he writes, "If I go up to the heavens [north], you are there; if I make my bed in the depths [south], you are there. If I rise on the wings of the dawn [the sun rises in the east], if I settle on the far side of the sea [now he's looking the other direction, which is west], even there your hand will guide me, your right hand will hold me fast." God is in front of us, he's behind us, he's above us, and he's below us. I think that covers it. He's everywhere all around us. David is singing, "Look at the matchless nature of God's presence!"

So if David has somehow laid hold of this truth so that he can sing about it, how can we have that same awareness? How can we grasp this dimension of God's nature so that it transforms our identity? To begin, let's think for a moment about what *omnipresence* is. Bill Bright defines it this way: "[Omnipresence] means that there is not a sliver of space anywhere in the universe where He is not dynamically and powerfully present with all of His wonderful personal attributes."[2] All of his nature—the entirety of the complexity of his being—is everywhere all the time.

Our problem with understanding this is that we tend to see it through our human eyes. We put human limitations on God. We think it would be great if we could be two places at once, let alone everywhere at once. We know we can't do it, so it seems impossible that God is able to. Well, God is not like us. We're finite; God is infinite. We're limited; God is unlimited. We are physical; God is spiritual. God's being is nothing like ours, thus when we let God be who God is—not spatially defined, but spiritually defined—then we start to understand. If God is the Creator of the universe as Genesis tells us, then it stands to reason that he is present everywhere in the world he has made.

More Than New Age Spiritualism

This is distinctly different from saying that God is present in everyone and everything. Such a view suggests that God is in the trees and the rocks and the wind and the music and in you and in me. Therefore all we have to do to connect to this mysterious presence is bang our drums, close our eyes, and chant a few lines, and voila! We have God's presence. No. God is present in creation, but the Bible tells us that his presence in our lives comes by faith.

The biblical story is this: As much as we yearn to be in the presence of God, we can't reach him no matter how many chants we chant or candles we burn. For that reason, God came down. God moved toward us through his incarnation in Jesus Christ. God's presence is uniquely born in us when we accept his cross-centered love and forgiveness. That's when we are filled by the Holy Spirit. That is wholly different from saying all people have the presence of God in them or that he is in the rocks and the flowers and the wind. Those elements reflect God's creative power, but he does not fill them. Yes, people reflect God's image because they have been made in God's image. Yes, the presence of God is around them, but the presence of God is not *in them* because God is not in relationship with them. The presence of God only inhabits those with whom he is in relationship.

Good News, Bad News

It is always important when exploring new truths to follow where those truths naturally lead. When we think about the implications of God's constant presence, if we're honest, it's a *good news, bad news* situation. The good news is that God is with us. We need not fear being alone, because we're not. The bad news is also that God is with us. Put more plainly, there is never a moment when God is not aware of what we are doing. See what I mean?

On the good news side, God's presence communicates loud and clear that he is not hiding from us. We can be lulled into falsely believing that God is in a cosmic game of hide-and-seek and he really doesn't want us to find him. We assume that in this sick game, God lures us down a road with the promise of his presence, but he never delivers, only teases us with the prospect. The obvious answer to the absurdity of such thought is Jesus. If God was trying to hide, then he never would have sent the fullest revelation of himself, namely, his Son. The very name of Jesus, Emmanuel, screams this truth: "God with us." Even Jesus's last words to his disciples reveal it: "I am with you always, even to the end of the age" (Matt. 28:20 NLT).

There has been an ad on TV lately for a company that describes the value of their organization as "the power of *with*." We're drawn to that. It feels good. We're attracted to it because we want someone to be with us. Well, if you want the ultimate power of *with*, then God says over and over and over again, "I am with you." Not only is it the meaning of Jesus's name, but God affirms several circumstances in which his presence can be found.

1. *He is with you when you seek to live obediently.* Paul writes in 1 Corinthians 10:13, "And God is faithful; he will not let you be tempted beyond what you can bear. But when you are tempted, he will also provide a way out so that you can endure it." When our hearts desire to follow Christ, he is powerfully present to show us his path even when the world is screaming at us to follow something else. He is always there to show us the way out. Our task is to quell the noise so we can hear him.

2. *He is with you when you are trying to speak words of comfort or of hope to another person.* When Moses feared that he would not speak the right words to Pharaoh, God said, "Now go; I will help you speak and will teach you what to say" (Exod. 4:12). Just as he told Moses that he would give him the words, so his presence inhabits our words. When we

speak his Word faithfully, it does not return void. Psalm 22:3 reminds us that God inhabits the praise of his people (see KJV). Thus God is with you as you live your life for him, as you speak his words, and as you worship.

3. *God is with you in times of trouble.* In Isaiah 43:1–2 God says, "Do not fear, for I have redeemed you; I have summoned you by name; you are mine. When you pass through the waters, I will be with you; and when you pass through the rivers, they will not sweep over you." God reaffirms this constantly in Scripture, and sometimes we have unique encounters with it in this life.

When I was a second-year seminary student in 1989, I was fighting an ongoing anxiety issue called panic disorder. I was functional but anxious and distracted because I could not eliminate irrational fears. My heart raced. I broke out in cold sweats. I had trouble concentrating. Sometimes I felt as though I had to run out of the room. Unless you've had a panic attack, the terror is hard to understand. Even so, I went to class, did my work, turned in my papers, ran a few miles, and ate dinner with my wife. That was my life. I didn't brave much more than that for fear of what might happen.

Midway through my second year, however, it began to dawn on me that there was an end to school. I was going to have to do an internship that summer, and then I would have to start looking for my first pastorate. The mere thought gripped me with more anxiety. I became more reclusive, more depressed, and more angry. I felt a deep rage at God that this state of depression and anxiety had become my fate. I cried out to him for months, praying for healing, praying for a sign that he was with me, and I got nothing. Zero.

As I looked at my future, I felt I had made a colossal mistake. Why was I even in seminary? I could never be a pastor in my present state. I could never hope to give a sermon in front of anyone. It was just not going to work. As the semester wore on, I started to think about what my life would be like working in some other field.

That spring I awoke one morning without much energy to do anything. Leigh did as she always did. She dressed and headed off to work managing a retail clothing store. I didn't have class until 10:00 a.m., so I lay there in bed thinking and praying about the state of my life. As I did, I noticed a light emanating from the hallway outside my bedroom. At first I thought it was the sun, but then I remembered that the morning sun was actually coming through the other window. The light continued to grow brighter and closer until I had to shield my eyes from it. While I could not look at it directly, there was an encompassing warmth as well.

Finally, this glorious light seemed to fully enter my room, and as it did, I was crushed into my bed. I know that sounds odd. It's odd for me to even write it, but that's the only way I know to describe it. It felt as though there were massive weights sitting on every inch of my body. I could not move. With my head mashed to the side, I struggled to look back at the glory. When I did, I saw the face of Jesus appear at the top of that light, and he said, "Help me." He repeated it three times. Then, suddenly, everything was gone.

The weight lifted and I sat up in my bed thinking, *What in the world was that? What just happened?* Very gently, the Holy Spirit confirmed a word from God to me in the depths of my heart. In no way did Jesus need my help. Far from it. That moment was God's revelation to me of his abiding presence in my call and that it was time to engage in his work. God was asking me to get in the game, to take part in what he was up to in the world.

As you can imagine, that day changed my life. It changed my life for two reasons: One, the overwhelming nature of

God's being cured my spiritual amnesia. I had made God so small in my own mind that I could not envision a way out of my anxiety disorder—or any other challenge for that matter. I experienced a microscopic sliver of his glory, and I suddenly remembered that God is glorious. Two, the experience also changed my life because I became profoundly aware of God's presence. I was not alone. I was not dealing with my issues by myself. This realization gave me a new sense of adequacy and confidence. I knew that no matter what I felt or what took place, God was right there *in all his glory*—and that was enough.

Now if you think God magically zapped away all my anxiety or that I never had another panic attack, you would be wrong. This is not one of those stories. However, God did give me the confidence to move forward, to open myself to the help of others, to trust in the abilities he had given me, and to walk more by faith than by sight. Slowly and steadily the anxiety went away. I learned the tools I needed to manage it. I learned how to lean into it and see the fears for what they were. As I walked through the doors he opened, God showed up every time, and he continues that faithfulness to this day.

You may also assume from this that I am always aware of God's presence. You would be wrong there too. I have had many times when God felt distant. Even so, the reality is that his presence in my life has never changed. He is always present. We do that as parents too. Sometimes we know our children really need us, but we also know that by removing our presence a bit, they learn. Swimming lessons is a great example. When our kids learned to swim, the parents were not allowed to stay during the lesson. Did that mean I left? Of course not. I was always peering through the fence making sure they were okay, but they didn't know that. They thought they were abandoned, but were they? No. I was right there.

Just because you don't *feel* God's presence does not mean he's not there.

The strange thing about my experience that spring morning is that I did not tell anyone about it for more than seven years. I thought that if I did, they would think I was some sort of weirdo. Don't misunderstand; I thought about it often. At times I convinced myself it was a dream. At other times I asked God for clarity. Finally, while journaling one morning, God slapped my hand a bit for assuming that moment was just for me. Wrong. He gave me that moment so I could proclaim the reality of his glorious presence, and I have been trying to do so ever since. I was fortunate to have that moment. I know that. You may be thinking, *Well, sure, I'd be more confident of God's presence if he showed up like that for me.* Remember, God has shown up for you. He showed up in Jesus, and for whatever reason, he sometimes takes weird, sinful people like me and reminds us of that. That's what it was—a reminder for all of us that he is right here with us.

His presence may be revealed to you in a supernatural way as it was once for me, or it may be revealed in an email or through a phone call or when you happen on a meaningful Scripture in your time with God or as you look on the wonder of his creation in a night sky. He is vast and far, and yet he is near and in you through Christ. Live in the knowledge of Emmanuel: God is with us.

The Bad News

I would be less than honest if I did not also discuss how God's presence can sometimes seem like bad news as well. The good news is that God is not hiding from you, but you also have to recognize that you can't hide from God. You may want to. You may think you can, but you can't. I think David has a good handle on this: "If I say, 'Surely the darkness will hide me and the light become night around me,' even the darkness will not be dark to you; the night will shine like the day, for darkness is as light to you" (Ps. 139:11–12). Ouch. Have you ever noticed that the things that we don't want anyone else to know we often do at night—burglaries and crimes, our secret internet sins, phone calls we make to people we should not be in relationship with—all of it.

We think that somehow the darkness will cover us—hide us—from others and ultimately from God. What God reveals, however, is that he is *in* the darkness, and when he's in it, the darkness becomes like daylight. I'll never forget getting a traffic ticket one night driving into Ft. Myers, Florida, on I-75. It was late in the evening, so when the policeman pulled me over with his lights flashing and his spotlight shining in my car, I felt like I was naked. My sinful speeding seemed to be illuminated for the whole world to see. Cars slowed and drivers looked as they passed. The word that kept coming to mind was *exposed*. I was praying the entire time that the policeman would hurry up so I could *get out of that light*.

We've all had the feeling. Exposure, especially when it comes to our poor choices or decisions, is never fun. But consider this: we want the light. We want the exposure, because in our gut what we do in darkness eats us alive, and if it hasn't already, it will. I'll never forget the haggard look on the face of a man as he came into my office. He looked awful. Over the next sixty minutes, he confessed that his wife had discovered his addiction to pornography. At one point he said, "I am so glad she found out. It was eating me alive. I needed help, but I couldn't bring myself to get it."

Similarly, a man caught in adultery by his wife said to me, "I knew it was a matter of time, and I was so relieved when she found out. The deception was killing me." As painful as it is, we need the light. We know what we do in darkness is dangerous, unhealthy, and destructive. We need that place to be illuminated so the purifying presence of God can clean it up and set us right.

Some of you reading this right now are living in darkness. You are trying to live without the presence of God because you have always denied the cross, denied his authority, and denied his love. Come out of that. Come into the light of his presence by faith. Ask God to shine the light of Christ into your life, and he will. He'll change you forever.

Others reading this are living by faith, but you also have dark, secret places hidden from view—places where you often linger. You think you can hide it, but the conviction of the Holy Spirit is falling on you to bring that to light—to stop what you're doing. You need to tell someone, "I got involved in this, but I need to get out. I have to bring some light to bear on this area of my life." It may be an extramarital affair. It may be a pornography addiction. It may be unethical behavior in your job. Regardless, what you think is bad news is actually good news. Bring it out into the light. You can't hide your sin from the presence of God—it will catch up to you eventually. Stop letting it eat you up, and allow his healing to begin in you. When you do, your identity will be determined by his presence, not by what you're hiding.

We Are God's Presence to Others

You may know the courageous story of Corrie ten Boom, who hid Jews during the Nazi occupation of her country in World War II. What we often don't know is that her sister, Betsie, worked alongside her. They saved countless lives, but they were eventually caught and sent to the prison camp at Ravensbruck. There they endured incredible deprivation, starvation, and humiliation. The suffering was tremendous, yet daily they ministered to others with the love and joy of their faith in Christ and the hope of his coming.

Eventually, Betsie became very ill and was taken to the prison hospital. In her last moments, Betsie told Corrie that she "must tell people what we have learned here. We must tell them that there is no pit so deep that He is not deeper still. They will listen to us, Corrie, because we have been there."[3] That is our fear isn't it? We fear we will find a pit so deep—a place so far—that God cannot reach us. We live with a constant anxiety that somehow we are alone in the world, a fear that drives us to stand in line for hours just so we can be hugged for thirty seconds by a woman we don't know.

The good news of the gospel is this: Our fears have been met in Jesus Christ. On the cross he descended into a pit deeper than any we will ever know—and he rose from it. His very name, Emmanuel, tells us that no matter where we are or what we face, God is with us. He will never leave us or forsake us. And then we have the joyful privilege of becoming his incarnational presence in the lives of others.

The church I currently serve endured a great tragedy shortly after I began my ministry here. One of our college students was killed in a car accident while driving back from Florida State University. He was a young man who loved the Lord, a young man with a bright future ahead of him. His death was devastating to many, but ever more so to his family. I'll never forget the long walk up to their house, pondering what I would say to this family I did not know. I would have completely understood if they had not wanted me to be there at all.

When I knocked on the door, however, I was greeted warmly and welcomed to walk with them in their loss. Yet what I remember most was what I saw once I entered the house. Every room was filled with people. In some there were conversations, in some people were praying, in others they sat quietly. In the ensuing days, I saw a family carried along by the presence of God made manifest through the presence of his people.

That is our privilege. That is our calling. God is spiritually present all the time, everywhere, in the fullness of his being. And you and I are the living, breathing witnesses to that fact. So let us be emboldened to look around us and see where that presence needs to be brought to bear.

Take heart. You are not alone. God is with you. Your true identity is found there.

7

Why Can't I Make Sense of My Life?

HOW THE KNOWLEDGE OF GOD TRANSFORMS OUR VIEW OF THE WORLD

You have searched me, LORD,
and you know me. . . .
Such knowledge is too wonderful for me,
too lofty for me to attain.

Psalm 139:1, 6

What matters supremely, therefore, is not, in the last analysis, the fact that I know God, but the larger fact which underlies it—the fact that He knows me.

J. I. Packer, *Knowing God*

I had been asleep for almost two hours when my pager went off. I bolted straight up, startled. Adrenaline is an amazing little chemical in our bodies, and I got a big shot of it at that moment. As part of my seminary training, I was a student chaplain at a Catholic hospital in Austin, Texas. I was one of six students serving internships that summer, and we took turns being on call through the night. Being on night call meant you slept on the sofa in the chaplain's office until you were paged to a room or to an emergency.

Because I was twenty-nine years old with no pastoral experience, every call made me nervous. I constantly had the overwhelming feeling that I did not know what I was doing, and the hard truth was that I didn't. The page came from Labor and Delivery, so I grabbed my Bible and my jacket and rushed downstairs.

When I arrived, I found a young woman in the middle of labor. While I did not know how long it had been going on, she looked as if she had just run a marathon. Her husband was dutifully at her side, calling out encouraging words and breathing instructions, but she seemed oblivious to any of that.

I introduced myself as a chaplain in the hospital, and they were immediately both relieved and grateful. They told me that they had just received news from the doctor that the baby was in distress, and they were unsure what to think. They were scared and wanted someone to pray for them and their baby. In the middle of all the chaos, with nurses coming in and out checking monitors, I offered a prayer. It was a meager attempt at comfort and supplication, but they seemed appreciative. I told them I would be outside if they needed me and stepped outside the room.

The next seventy minutes were a whirlwind of raw human experience—moments that remain indelibly etched in my mind. As I stood outside the room, doctors were called. Two came to the room, then a third. Nurses came in as well. As I watched, the team wheeled her from the room into a surgical suite, her husband following close behind. And in minutes, it was over. The cord had been wrapped around the child's neck, and in the lengthy process of labor, he had slowly strangled. Their son never took a breath outside her womb.

I had encountered death before, but never this kind of death, never something this profoundly unfair. It seemed utterly senseless. The couple was distraught to their core, speaking occasionally, but mostly sobbing in each other's arms as various nurses took care of the mother's physical needs. I stood there trying to lend support, but mentally I was lost in an abyss of spiritual confusion.

Then suddenly, and without warning, the mother started struggling to breathe. Her face became pale and then covered in sweat. Her husband ran for help. I excused myself and waited outside as staff members rushed to her side. A code was called. Crash carts arrived. Sounds of rushed, frantic movement spilled into the hallway where I stood. And just like that, she too was gone. I was told that in the labor process, amniotic fluid had escaped the womb, traveled to her heart, and stopped it. It was an extraordinarily rare occurrence, but there it was nonetheless.

I stood with the husband trying to quell my rising sense of panic. Everything in me wanted to run out of the room, because I felt as though some of my personal faith foundations were crumbling. I wanted someone to shake me and wake me from this horrific nightmare, but that shaking never came. It was real—coldly, brutally real.

In the ensuing hours, I did what I could. Along with several members of the medical staff, I escorted the father to a family room so he could gather himself. His family and his wife's family were from other parts of the country, so they were not there. It was the middle of the night, so friends had not come. He was all alone. Still, forms had to be signed. A funeral home had to be called to arrange for the disposition of the bodies. Family members and friends needed to be contacted. Without expression, he soldiered on, calling, signing, telling. Through it all, I feebly prayed with him from time to time. I helped make some calls. I brought him food and a soda.

Finally, with those tasks accomplished, he was ready to leave the hospital. I accompanied him to the door, expressed my deep sympathy, and watched him walk toward the parking lot, the sun rising ahead of him. There I stood, the new day dawning, watching a man who had entered the hospital full of joy and anticipation, leaving completely and unalterably alone. To this day, it is the saddest thing I have ever witnessed.

My hours complete, I was free to go home, but I could not. I sat on the bench outside the entrance and sank into an emotional haze. It made no sense. No matter how hard I tried or how much Scripture I quoted to myself, I did not know what to do. I did not know how to make sense of what had just happened to this family. I kept asking God, "How does this fit with what I know to be true about you? How does this make sense in your plan?"

In the days that followed, I worked with my chaplain supervisor to process my feelings. I wrote in my journal. I prayed. And over time, I gradually learned. I grew in my faith. No, I never understood the event, but I did understand another important truth: my knowledge of this life is limited. For each of us there are experiences, events, and circumstances that we will never understand. We will never know, this side of heaven, why they happened, other than the fact that we live in a sinful, fallen world that often affects our lives.

That, of course, leads to another question: If there are things we do not know and cannot know, then is there anyone who does? That's important, because if I can't figure out what's going on, and no one else knows either, then I will be deeply insecure and anxious about my life. Such a conclusion can only leave us feeling as though life is nothing more than a runaway train heading for disaster.

It is for this reason that this chapter is so important. There is someone who knows—God does. Not only does he know about what happened in that hospital all those years ago, but he knows what happened yesterday, he knows what will happen today, and he knows what will happen tomorrow and beyond.

Further, his knowledge goes beyond mere awareness. God knows not only what is happening in our lives but also how it fits. We may not understand everything, but he knows how he wants to use what has taken place in our lives for his greater plan and purpose. Events are not disconnected, meaningless occurrences. They are known by God and used for his greater glory.

Our ability to know and understand this dimension to God's nature—his *omniscience*—can transform how we see both our personal world and our larger world. Our understanding of God's nature as omniscient allows us to make sense of our lives in ways that we could otherwise never imagine. If we don't know everything, then we need to know the one who does so that the confusion and chaos of this life does not send us into a spiral of doubt and despair.

Our Fascination with Knowledge

Some years ago I was perusing the pages of our local newspaper when I came across an interesting story about a young man named Santhosh Balasubramanian. The story described his status as a senior at Timber Creek High School; his participation in debate, orchestra, and tennis; and his coming entrance into Stanford University. The purpose of the story was to announce that Mr. Balasubramanian had achieved a perfect score on his SAT exam—a 2400. On this rigorous college entrance examination, he knew the answer to every single question on the test. Either that or he guessed really well.

I was also amazed to discover that he was one of only ninety-seven others who had perfect scores on the exam among the 90,000 students who took it. Reading this, of course, reminds me of my own SAT experience. As much as my parents tried to help me, after three tries I had to resign myself to the fact that I just didn't know as much as others who took the test.

I have managed to do fairly well in life without a perfect SAT score, but I certainly admire people who are smart—people who know a lot. I grew up with a sister who was number two in her high school class and Phi Beta Kappa in college. She is now a medical doctor. I used to look at her textbooks and think, *How does she know all that?* I admire people like George Atwell, organist and composer for our church. If it makes a noise or has a key, George knows how to play it, and play it beautifully. I admire people like Joe Alexander, one of our elders, who has memorized more Scripture than I have ever dreamed of—Scripture that flows off his lips in prayer and conversation as a blessing of God to others.

This same interest in knowledge also fuels our interest in game shows, doesn't it? We watch *Are You Smarter than a Fifth Grader?* to see if we are. We blurt out the answers before the contestants so we can feel smug about how much we know. There's a part of us that wants to know—that wants to be smart. In these past years, however, I have discovered a few things about this whole concept of knowledge. In spite of my best efforts to know a lot, it seems I actually know less. The more I learn, the more I find there is to know.

I live with three teenagers who seem to think I get dumber with each passing year, reinforcing this point. Even so, I have also learned this: no one knows everything. A scientist may know a lot about the intricacy of the human body but nothing about literature. A writer may know great things about prose but nothing about human history. A historian may know numerous details about history but nothing about the Dallas Cowboys. Tony Romo may know a lot about playing quarterback for the Dallas Cowboys but nothing about reading Latin. I think you see my point. There is no one who knows everything. Or is there? Is it possible that we worship an omniscient God—an all-knowing God? And if he is omniscient, how is that good news?

An All-Knowing God

In trying to understand this truth, we are helped enormously by Psalm 139. It is one of the most widely known of all the psalms of David. It speaks to God's power as Creator, telling us in verse 14 that we are "fearfully and wonderfully made." As great as that is, David is trying to accomplish more in this text than just improve our self-esteem. It is actually a poem that was used as a song of worship that helped the people of Israel remember particular attributes of God.

If God made all things, then logically we can assume he has complete knowledge of those things. He knows all about what he made, including us. That's also true in our lives. What we make, we know. If I take all the elements needed and build an engine for a car, I am going to know all the dynamics of that engine. If I paint a landscape scene, I am going to know everything about that painting. God, as Creator, knows intimately what he has made. He knows the vast nature of the heavens and the earth, the intricacies of quantum physics and imploding stars, not to mention the way birds fly and how the wind blows. He also knows our thoughts even before we have them. He knows when we lie down and when we get up. He knows what we are going to say before we say it. In Psalm 139:6 David declares, "Such knowledge is . . . too lofty for me to attain." In other words, David cannot comprehend the extent of the knowledge of God. There is no one like him. So in light of what we find in Psalm 139, what do we learn?

To begin, I want you to understand that our desire for knowledge is part of our sinful nature and the root of our downfall. I know that sounds negative in a way, so let me explain. Pursuing the knowledge of what God has made, knowledge that leads us to a deeper understanding of him, is a wonderful thing. Cultivating the gift of our minds is something that honors God, but the arrogant or prideful pursuit of knowledge, largely for the sake of personal power, is grounded in our sinful nature. Like the psalmist, we stand back and say, "Wow, God, no one knows as much as you do—but I'd like to. I'd like to be like you." Therefore we pursue knowledge. We even try to kid ourselves that we actually know as much as God, that we can be god to ourselves in matters of choice.

We do this all the time. In matters of personal morality and sexual behavior, in matters of finance and speech, in matters of ethics—we proudly think we know better. Even though God says something to the contrary, we dismiss it because we think we know more than God does. We know what is best for us. Let's look back at the second chapter of Genesis. Verse 9 says, "In the middle of the garden were the tree of life and the tree of the knowledge of good and evil." God commands, "You are free to eat from any tree in the garden; but you must not eat from the tree of the knowledge of good and evil, for when you eat from it you will certainly die" (vv. 16–17). Knowing us as he does, God says, "If you start to think you know more than you do, if you start wanting to act like me—wanting to pretend that you know good and evil—you will perish. Such pursuit will wreck you—crush you."

We are crushed by it because who alone truly knows good and evil? Who among us has the capacity for that? Can any of us truly say we are capable of being the judge of what is good and what is evil? I never want to be in that position because I don't know. I don't know what is completely just. I don't know what people deserve. I don't know how one action compares to another, especially given that I can never know the heart or thoughts of another. Who are we kidding?

Even so, it still tempts us, doesn't it? We want to think we know what's good. We want to say to the Lord, "Well God, thanks for your advice, but *I* really know what is best. I'm going to reject what you say and do what I think I should do." We seem to think that God can't know more than we do.

When we start to think that way, God says *we will surely die.* We have eaten that fruit, and the result has been disaster. We see this in our own lives just by examining the way people talk. We want to know things, so we pump others for information about what they know, and then we love to talk about what we know, even if it's not totally true. The root of our sinful gossip is found in our desire to be *in the know*. It gives us power, which is why we reach for that fruit. We think we can know what only God knows, but we can't.

Trusting God's Perfect Knowledge

In light of that, we must yield to the truth that only God has perfect knowledge. That's what the psalmist means when he says God is "behind and before" (Ps. 139:5). God's knowledge is complete. First John 3:20 says that God knows everything.

In this computer age, I find the amount of knowledge that we have access to astounding, and it just keeps increasing. Today the most sophisticated computers can perform 32 billion calculations per second and can store a billion characters in their memories, but that's not good enough.

Information is amassing so fast that computer experts are close to building a network that can do one trillion calculations per second—a measure known as a teraflop. Yet here's the thing: even then, we won't have reached the end of it. Even the most powerful computers still won't be able to know everything. It just keeps going. Bill Bright writes, "Most scientists spend their lives trying to understand the mysteries of life and the universe. But for our all-knowing God, there are no mysteries. He has a clear understanding of everything that baffles mankind. To him, a teraflop is nothing."[1] God's knowledge is unfathomable. It's too lofty for us to attain. In light of that, shouldn't we yield to it? Shouldn't we lay down the burden of having to know and yield to the knowledge of God revealed in Jesus Christ?

When we do that, our lives begin to be transformed. That's what makes a difference in how we see our world and how we make sense of our circumstances. In that hospital when the baby and mother died, I didn't know why, but I learned to trust in the one who does. I had to yield my lack of knowledge to his all-encompassing knowledge and trust in his goodness and love. In doing so, the burden of those moments and my inability to make sense of them gradually lifted. It has been a principle I have leaned on many times since. As a pastor, I often encounter the senseless things of this world. If I did not trust that God knows what is happening and is at work through it, I would never be able to sleep at night. I could not go on. However, because I do believe in God's omniscience, I move forward with confidence, assured that while I don't know, he does.

I am not saying that God wants us to be ignorant. I am not saying that we are incapable of any knowledge—far from it. Will we have all knowledge? No. Can we have some knowledge? Absolutely. James 1:5 says, "If any of you lacks wisdom, you should ask God, who gives generously to all." We can't know everything, but God wants us to know what we need—what will help us in this life. So ask. Our knowledge is imperfect and always will be, but God's is perfect, complete. In this life, there are some things I'm just not going to understand or figure out. Thus God's omniscience is life changing and reassuring! Let him start being the fountain of wisdom and knowledge in your life. Start doing what he says—following what he knows—and that will bring blessing to your life.

Good News!

God's perfect knowledge is good news for us. David says in Psalm 139:6, "Such knowledge is too wonderful for me." When David grasped one small part—one iota—of the knowledge of God, it filled him with wonder. He was thrilled at the prospect because he realized that in the vastness of the universe, there *is* someone who knows. With all that is unknown and confusing, the fact that there *is* someone who knows is exceedingly good news.

When I come to terms with how little I know, I *want* God to know everything because I need to know that things are not spinning out of control. I need to know that if I don't know, there is someone trustworthy who does. Charles Spurgeon writes, "Our paths may be habitual or accidental, open or secret, but with them all the Most Holy One is well acquainted. This should fill us with awe so that we sin not; with courage, so that we fear not; and with delight so that we mourn not."[2]

119

Do you see? The fact that God knows everything is great news! It should fill us with such a sense of awe and reverence that it changes our behavior. It should convict us that we cannot do anything that God does not know about. So let's stop kidding ourselves and start being obedient.

Isn't it funny how we do that? We love to believe that there are secret places and secret sins that we can keep all to ourselves. We love to believe that these vices can be protected and held without the interference of others, or even of God. I do it. You do it. We all do it. But it's not reality. He knows! You cannot hide it, even in darkness. So the better choice for us is to embrace what his omniscience reveals: God is always aware of our behavior and actions, so living faithfully in the awareness of that knowledge is actually what sets us free. For example, I have never heard an unfaithful spouse say to me, "Wow, that affair was so worth it!" To the contrary, they often describe the agonizing guilt and pain of living a double life. The discovery of the affair is often met with a sense of relief. The secrecy eats them alive. Further, it is only when the sin was brought to light that they were delivered, set free, from the burden of what they were doing. We may live under the illusion, for a time, that we can do things in secret, but the secret will consume us until we bring it to the light of God's ultimate knowledge.

His omniscience should also fill us with courage, because whatever we face, God knows about it. He is not shocked or surprised by what is happening to you. You may be faced with a great unknown, but your courage in facing it is born from your understanding that God knows about it. He knows, and if he knows and he loves you and he has a plan for your life, then there is an element of confidence and courage that is derived no matter what the situation. Again drawing from my experience in the hospital, my courage to go on after that day was born out of my trust in God's knowledge. I didn't want to encounter any other patients, trust me. But I had to get past my own lack of knowledge and take courage from God's complete knowledge—he knows what he is doing, he is good, he loves me, and he will answer all things in the end.

It's also good news because it changes our view of what happens to us. We endure things in this life that knock us down, that pain us, and that wound us. There are things that happen that confuse us, things we don't understand. Our common response is often, "God, where were you? Why did you let this happen?" Instead, we can find peace in knowing that while we may not understand it, God does. As long as someone knows, and that someone is loving and trustworthy, then we can move forward with courage and confidence. It does not mean we won't hurt, but it does relieve us of the burden of having to make it fit together neatly. God knows about it, and if he knows, then I must trust him, because there are some things that I cannot know.

Unfortunately, that's not our typical response. Instead, we often believe that if we can't come up with a good explanation for why something happened, there must not be one. We reach up into heaven and pull God down to our level and in effect say, "God, you are no smarter than I am, because I can't figure this out." Don't you think it's possible that God may be up to something to which you're not privy? Of course! God knows things you don't know, and if we trust that instead of fighting it, we cease mourning and welcome joy.

For example, look at John 11 when Mary and Martha call for Jesus to come help their dying brother, Lazarus. What happens? He doesn't get there in time. Does he know what is happening? Yes, he does. When he finally arrives, Martha runs down the road to meet him and asks him point-blank,

"Where were you? Why didn't you get here?" It made no sense to them.

Interestingly, Jesus never answers those questions. He never explains why he delayed. He does not try to help them make sense of it. He does, however, *grieve* with them. He identifies with their suffering, and then he brings life. He will always bring life. Jesus knew exactly what he was doing. He knew the situation, and he was faithful. Did Mary and Martha understand it all? No, but I imagine they learned to trust in God's greater knowledge as a result of the experience. God's omniscience is good news because it changes not only how we see our world but also how we see our life, our experiences, and our circumstances.

How God Knows Us

Finally, as good as that is, in the end I think the most important thing is what Psalm 139 really emphasizes. Yes, God knows all things, but that knowledge is on a very personal, intimate level. David says in verse 1, "You have searched me, Lord, and you know me." Yes, God knows all things, but more important, he knows me and he knows you. We are fully known by God. J. I. Packer writes:

> What matters supremely, therefore, is not, in the last analysis, the fact that I know God—but the larger fact that underlies it—the fact that He knows me. I am graven on the palms of His hands. I am never out of His mind; and there is no moment where His eye is off me, or His attention distracted from me, and no moment, therefore, when His care falters.[3]

I think that's what we want. We want someone we can know, but even more than that, we yearn for someone to know us—our thoughts, feelings, gifts, failures, and flaws—and in knowing all that, still love us. That's exactly what God does, and that's the good news of the gospel.

Prevalent in our world today is the growing problem of identity theft. We work diligently to protect information that is unique to our personal identity—information that could be used to hurt us or steal from us in some way. There are people out there who can use their computer knowledge to literally steal who we are. Then they can take their knowledge of us and use it against us.

On a smaller scale, we fear the same thing in our personal relationships. The reason we guard our hearts so closely, the reason we don't want others to know about our past, is our fear that they will take that knowledge and use it against us. We fear that if others have complete knowledge of us, they will not like us. So we are extraordinarily careful about what we allow others to know.

We need never fear this with God. He knows everything about us and loves us in spite of it. Further, God will *never* use his complete knowledge against us. He knows our past. "While we were still sinners, Christ died for us" (Rom. 5:8). Before we even understood we were a mess, he loved us and died for us. And he knows our future. "'I know the plans I have for you,' declares the LORD, 'plans to prosper you and not to harm you'" (Jer. 29:11). And with all that knowledge, he loves us sacrificially and eternally.

Who You Know

In Jeremiah 9:23–24, God declares, "Let not the wise boast of their wisdom or the strong boast of their strength or the rich boast of their riches, but let the one who boasts boast about this: that they have the understanding to know me, that I am the LORD." I have found something to be true in life that is said in many circles: it's not what you know, but who you know.

When I was trying to get into colleges, I found it was helpful if I knew someone to offset my demonstrated lack of knowledge on the SAT exam. I asked my parents to connect me with anyone they knew who had attended the university I was applying to. I made phone calls. I asked their contacts to write letters on my behalf. And I got an interview in the admissions office. No question, those contacts helped.

Several years ago I was invited by United States senator Bill Nelson to be Chaplain for the Day in the United States Senate, which included giving the opening prayer on the floor of the Senate. Senator Nelson was a tremendous host and shepherded me around the facility most of the day. What I noticed was the marvelous access that I had because I knew him. We went into elevators marked "Senators only." We ate in a dining room that was "Senators only." We rode an underground train that was for "Senators only." Each time I started to move into one of these restricted areas, Senator Nelson looked at the guard or attendant and said, "He's my guest." In other words, "I know him. He's with me." I could have known copious amounts about the United States government or public policy, but it would not have mattered. The only thing that mattered in the Senate chambers was *who* I knew and who knew me.

In the final analysis, the only thing that really matters is not what we know or what we knew in this life. What matters is *who* we know—and who knows us. When I stand at the gates of heaven, God will not ask for my exam scores. He will not ask about what I knew in life. He will not ask me whether I ever understood what happened in the hospital that day. He will not ask me if I was able to explain flawlessly to my congregation certain aspects of Scripture or theology. He will only ask, "Did you know me?" In that moment, it won't be what I know but who knows me. Praise God, he knows me.

And he knows you. He knows everything about you and loves you still. My prayer is that you will let go of your need to figure out all your circumstances and experiences—an endeavor that will leave you only more frustrated and anxious. I pray that you will stop trusting in your own knowledge and trust in the wonder of God's omniscience. As you do, may it fill you with peace, courage, and purpose as you live out your life day by day, no matter what happens. May your understanding of his omniscience change how you see your world, because ultimately, God knows. God knows what he's doing.

8

How Can I Get Rid of My Baggage?

FINDING THE FREEDOM TO LET GO

If you hold to my teaching, you are really my disciples. Then you will know the truth, and the truth will set you free.

John 8:31–32

Freedom lies in being bold.

Robert Frost

It had already been a rather long day when the phone rang in my hotel room at 11:15 p.m. I was in Orange County, California, instead of Florida, so my body felt like it was 2:15 a.m. I had flown in that morning, along with my good friend and fellow Orlando pastor William Andrews, to make a presentation about our HIV/AIDS ministry at the

Saddleback Global AIDS Conference. We endured a long flight, raced to the church, made our presentation, shared in follow-up conversations, grabbed some dinner, and then finally headed to our hotel. Like I said, I was tired.

When I picked up the phone, Kay Warren was on the other end. She apologized for calling so late, but she said she had an important opportunity to discuss with me. As he often does, Rick Warren, Saddleback's pastor, had invited all the 2008 presidential candidates to come to the conference to address the problem of AIDS in the world as well as a host of other social issues. With one exception, the candidates sent videos that were played during the event. The one exception was then Senator Hillary Clinton, now our secretary of state. She accepted his invitation to come in person.

Senator Clinton was scheduled to speak the next morning, but she had asked Kay Warren for a meeting with a small group of pastors in order to better understand our perspective on a variety of topics. Kay was calling to ask if William and I would like to be in that group. Naturally, we said yes.

The next morning, we were taken to a small room just off the main platform where the senator would speak. We met briefly with her staff person responsible for the religion and values portion of her campaign, and then we waited. As a means of context, her campaign had been in full swing for six months, and at the time, she was the clear frontrunner over a group of candidates that included a relative newcomer named Barack Obama.

When she entered the room, I was immediately struck by a rather ridiculous insight: she was a real human being. It's funny how we act sometimes, isn't it? We see people on television or read about them in the newspaper, and we think we know them. We relate to them based on their ideologies or words, their actions or decisions, while failing to appreciate that they are ordinary human beings just like us. We make them caricatures of themselves instead of real people.

Senator Clinton was a real human being, and she looked very tired. In spite of that, as she spoke to the four of us, she could not have been more gracious and kind. She warmly invited our ideas and opinions, eagerly asked questions about our churches and our ministries, and shared honestly from her faith perspective on some of the same matters we addressed. As we concluded, she seemed genuinely grateful that we had taken the time to meet with her.

Perhaps it was the pastoral side of me coming out, but I could not shake my feelings regarding the overwhelming nature of the burdens she carried. I couldn't imagine the schedule she was keeping, the amount of information she had to retain in her mind, the myriad number of cities she was in every week, the countless speeches she had to give, the ridiculous hours she worked while being constantly separated from friends and family—all as an expression of her desire to lead the country. In that moment, all of it appeared as if it were resting squarely on her shoulders.

I suspect that any Christian in that moment, regardless of his or her political views, would have been moved as I was. Every part of me wanted to say something encouraging to her. I wanted to ask her if I could pray for her or do something for her. Because of the setting and the strict schedule, such opportunity was limited, but I did get to express my concern for her as she left us to go on stage. The four of us watched her speech from that same back room, and then we stepped outside the rear entrance where her motorcade had assembled.

Four black SUVs waited, engines idling. Secret Service agents surrounded the perimeter. Soon Senator Clinton emerged with Kay Warren, smiled, waved to us one more time, and then got into one of the SUVs by herself. Agents closed the door, glanced quickly at each other, and then got in their vehicles. A few minutes later, all four vehicles sped away.

As William and I stood there, I remember sharing some of my feelings with him. How does a person in her position manage such a load, especially when she has to do so in the absence of any support network of family and friends? She was soldiering on, but I thought, *How in the world does she ever find ways to put all those burdens—that baggage—down?*

The more I thought about it, the more I realized it was a good question to ask myself. I'm not a candidate for president, and you're probably not either, but that does not mean that the burdens of your life are insignificant. They are your burdens. They are my burdens. They are the bags we carry, and they impact our lives. If we can't find ways to deal with those bags and burdens—if we can't find ways to free ourselves from the weight—then ultimately, they will crush us.

Everybody Has a Bag or Two

No doubt our burdens take on many forms. They're all different, but all of us have bags we carry. For the past five years, my two sons have played basketball for Winter Park High School. As many teams do, we travel for some tournaments and games, and each boy has a Winter Park travel bag. They all look identical: black with a WP logo on one side. On trips, they are all packed full. The challenge, of course, is finding the right bag when they come through baggage claim. Some boys learned to put an identifying marker on their bag, but some did not. In those cases, you would see boys unzipping bags and looking at the contents in order to ensure they got the proper one. Everyone had a bag, but each bag was unique in its contents.

So it is with us. No one comes through life without a bag. God never promised that. He said we would have troubles and burdens and challenges. We all have bags, but the burdens inside are different. Some of us carry the weight of troubled childhoods or past abusive relationships. Some of us carry the weight of past failures or poor decisions. Some of us carry the wounds of broken relationships. Some of us carry the grief of lost loved ones. Some of us carry the burden of disease or physical infirmity. Some of us carry the burden of financial stress or even ruin. Some of us carry the burden of emotional illness or aging parents or unmet expectations or relentless addictions. The list of things in our bags could go on and on. The contents of our bags are different, but we all have burdens we carry.

While God did not promise us a life without burdens, he did give us some clues about how to find freedom from those burdens. Yet many of us never figure that out. We live like the people we see in airports, hauling multiple bags around wherever they go—restaurants, bookstores, bathrooms, everywhere. They don't want to pay the fee to check them, so they wander about totally encumbered—and exhausted. It's a great picture of our lives. I often want to go up to those people and say, "Just put them down. Put them down."

John 11 gives us a good picture of this as well. Lazarus has died. In spite of Mary and Martha's call for Jesus to come, he does not make it in time. In fact, when Jesus finally arrives, not only is Lazarus dead, but he's in the grave. Undeterred, Jesus prays and then calls out, "Lazarus, come out!" Then "the dead man came out, his hands and feet wrapped with strips of linen, and a cloth around his face. Jesus said to them, 'Take off the grave clothes and let him go'" (vv. 43–44).

Lazarus is dead, but Jesus brings him back to life. What's the problem? He's still bound up. He's not free. Jesus has to instruct those near Lazarus to unwrap the strips of linen—the "grave clothes"—so that he can "go." Essentially, Jesus says to those around Lazarus, "Set him free from what binds him." What a great image for so many of us. We've been brought back to life by Jesus. We have been redeemed from the darkness of our sin, and we have entered into the love and grace of God. We're free! I believe that is part of our true identity. We are not slaves. We are to live as free men and women according to the love and grace of God.

Sadly, we don't. We're alive in Christ, but we're still bound up. We live in bondage instead of the freedom God promises. Our true identity becomes trapped under the weight of the bags we carry. We look for places to set them down. We look for ways to find relief, but either we can't find them or we become so comfortable in our misery that we refuse to put down our bags. Our identity becomes what we carry, not the person we are as one set free in Christ.

In light of those challenges, what do we do? How can we get free from all our bags? How can we learn to put them down and find freedom in life so we can truly live?

Yearning for Freedom

Several years ago I had an experience that pushed me outside my comfort zone. It was sort of like taking a mission trip without ever leaving home. I went with a group of ten men to visit and teach the male inmates at our local county jail. If you have never been to such a facility, I highly recommend the experience. One of the first things you notice is the intensity of the security. There are guards everywhere, and they all look intimidating. You don't feel much like cracking jokes or smiling.

We entered one room and went through metal detectors, leaving our personal belongings behind. We then walked outside and into another building where we had to step in front of a camera so those in the control booth could see our badges. At that point, the huge metal door in front of us jerked and slowly rolled open. We all stepped forward into a long concrete hallway, and then we heard the door behind us roll shut. It made a jarring sound as the locks slammed into place. The noise echoed down the hallway as if to remind us where we were.

Admittedly, I was anxious, and then I realized why. There was something profoundly different about how the jail worked compared to everything else in my life. In all the other areas of my life, I want to be secure. Security is important. Like you, I create security by putting locks on things. We have locks on our doors, our windows, our cars, our bathrooms. My goodness, until I had teenagers, I never knew how many of the doors in my house actually had locks. Locking our doors makes us feel secure, but where are those locks located? The locks on our doors are on the *inside*. Not so at the jail. When I heard that door lock shut, I suddenly realized that the locks in that place were on the outside. I began to feel acutely anxious when it dawned on me that if I wanted to get out of that place fast, I couldn't. I was locked in.

At some level, we're all that way, aren't we? We yearn to be free, but we can't find the lock. We all want to be unencumbered. We want to be able to do what we want when we want. Freedom is one of the great virtues in our country. How many times have you heard, "I live in a free country"? Yet what is freedom really? Webster's dictionary defines it: "the quality or state of being free; the absence of necessity, coercion, or constraint; liberation from slavery or restraint or from the power of another."[1] Based on that definition, the question is: Does the absence of constraint make us truly free? Is that all there is to it?

Let me give you a couple of examples: An eighteen-year-old high school senior buys a truck and gets a job to pay for the gas and insurance. Everything he makes goes into that vehicle. He decides he wants new rims for his tires, so four months short of graduation he drops out of school to be able to work more hours. His parents plead with him to reconsider, but his response is, "I'm eighteen. I'm free to do what I want." Was that young man really free, or was he enslaved?

A forty-two-year-old man, married for twenty-one years with three children, finds a co-worker who really understands him. She's young and vivacious, and she makes him feel attractive. He leaves his wife and kids to move in with his new love. When confronted by his pastor, he says, "I'm free to do what I want." Was that man free, or was he a slave? What does it mean to be truly free, and where do we find freedom?

Some say faith or religion is the last place to look. Christopher Hitchens argues that religion was originally created by human beings to control others, not to set them free.[2] Michael Onfray writes, "It all began with that ancient lesson from Genesis: man is forbidden to seek awareness."[3] In other words, faith in God is about rules that bind you and keep you from being aware of what life really offers. God is trying to prevent your freedom. And that is what often keeps people away from Christian faith. They think God is up there trying to tie their hands, not free them. So like the serpent who whispered in Eve's ear in Genesis 3, we hear the voices of our time saying, "Really, it's fine. Ignore what you have heard about God. He's not really like that. You need to eat the fruit. Live for yourself. Making your own decisions is what makes you truly free." But does it?

Finding True Freedom

God has some rather important things to say on that topic, so let's take a look at John 8 to find some answers. It stands to reason that if we want to live out of our identity as those who have been freed in Christ rather than being bound or defined by our burdens, then we need to understand the origins of that freedom—the source of that freedom. Rest assured, we are not the first ones to wrestle with this question. People have been bound up since the dawn of time. The search for freedom has been a constant drumbeat in the human experience, and it was no different in Jesus's day. The Jews lived under the heaviness of religion and the burden of having to keep a virtually impossible law. It was overwhelming, and each day they failed. They lived under the constant burden of never measuring up to the requirements of the law. Thus their faith was not a joy or an encouragement. Instead, they tried to figure out some way to be delivered from the weight of the system.

Imagine, then, their curiosity when Jesus appears on the scene and starts doing miracles and declaring that God is his Father. The people are intrigued enough to investigate. Can this man be the Messiah—the path to freedom? Jesus says, "If you hold to my teaching, you are really my disciples. Then you will know the truth, and the truth will set you free" (John 8:31–32). Jackpot. There it is. There's the key. Knowing the truth makes us free. So if I want to be free, I have to find the truth. Guess what? You know that too.

God is truth. God's nature is truth. The core element of his being is all that is true and right. There is nothing in him that is false or misleading or coercive. Jesus affirms this in John 14:6 when he says, "I am the way and the truth and the life." He is the standard by which we make that determination, and that standard never changes. In our world, however, quite the opposite is upheld. We are told that truth is relative. Truth is not determined by one objective standard but instead by the subjective measure of each individual.

Think about how that works in real life. Does that actually make sense? There are things that are always, absolutely true. How do we mark time? The absolute standard for time is Greenwich Mean Time. No one disputes that. Can you imagine what would happen if we allowed the airline industry to set time based on their preference? Chaos. What if we allowed individual civil engineers to determine their own standard for weights and measures? Everything would collapse. Roads and buildings would fail because the absolute standard for measurements had not been followed. We say there are no absolute truths, yet we depend each day on absolute truths to keep our world from imploding. Why would it be any different in the spiritual realm?

Richard Dawkins provides the generally accepted cultural answer. He says in *The God Delusion* that the only standard for truth is what science reveals quantifiably along with what can be learned from the natural world around us. According to Dawkins, this is the only way we can know true reality. He says it is through new instruments that allow our senses to perceive new data that we discover new truth. It is curious, however, that he denies our physical senses when it comes to our awareness of God but affirms them when it comes to understanding science or true reality. And that's just it: Who has made these new machines? We have. Who interprets their data? We do. Thus those machines are vulnerable to the same problems as our limited senses because we create them and we interpret their data. Sense perception can be fooled, so what we think may be true, because we are far from perfect, may in fact be false.

Dawkins writes, "The human brain runs first-class simulation software."[4] In other words, we can't trust our senses, because our brains train us to simulate what we want to be true. We create our own reality. However, that's the very thing that defeats his argument. Even with the best instruments, the most reliable data, the purest environment, our faulty senses may see only what we want to see and not what is, in fact, true. Even in the scientific realm, it still goes back to us—our senses, our judgment, and our machines. If we're faulty, how can we always assume our senses, perceptions, and interpretations will not be? We can't. Most of the time scientists get it right, but they are not the standard for truth. What we need is a standard that lies outside of ourselves, and that standard for truth is the one who is completely true in his nature—our living God revealed in Jesus Christ. He is the truth, and thankfully, he is knowable.

Truth and Freedom

If freedom is found in knowing truth, and God is truth, and we know God, then we've uncovered some excellent news. We're almost there. There is a magnificent, indelible link between truth and freedom. Jesus says in John 8:32, "Then you will know the truth, and the truth will set you free." We all want to be free, right? What makes us free? Truth. Who is truth? God. Which tells us what? The lock that keeps us in bondage is not on the outside; it's on the inside. Freedom is within our grasp. All we have to do to get free is to live according to the truth that God has revealed—that is the key. Newsflash: the reason so many people live in bondage is because they refuse to use the key or they don't understand the key or they deny the key. That eighteen-year-old boy thought freedom was in that truck. That forty-two-year-old man thought freedom was in that younger woman. They ignored the key offered in Christ for one of their own choosing, but their keys didn't fit the door. Like them, we are bound up by our own choices. As long as we refuse the truth offered us in Christ, the door to our freedom never opens.

One of the things I enjoy most about my job is visiting hospitals. On days when the organization and administration of ministry becomes tedious and draining, going to the hospital allows me to connect with people. However, getting around in hospitals can be tricky sometimes. There are signs that say "Doctors only," which is great for me since I am a doctor. I'm not a medical doctor, but I do have a doctorate, so in the absence of any further questioning on that subject, I go right through those doors. There are also doors that have security codes and have to be opened from the inside. Getting out is easy. There's a little green button to the side of the door that says, "Push to Exit." You push the button, you hear the door release, and out you go.

One day I was leaving and I came upon a middle-aged man about to rip the door off the hinges. He was furious because he couldn't get out. I said, "Sir, can I help you with that?" In a loud voice, he started verbally attacking the nurse, saying, "She said I could get out down here—she doesn't know what she's talking about—she's blah blah blah. . . ." I said, "Sir, if you'll allow me, I think I can help. All you need to do is push that little green button right there that says 'Push to Exit.'" With that he stopped midrant and saw the button. He reached down and pushed it. The door released. Needless to say, he felt a bit foolish. The key to getting out was right there. It was even labeled, but he missed it.

That's a good picture of how we live at times. So many people are bound up and mad because they can't get free. They desperately try to let go of the burdens and the bags, but they can't figure it out. They try to rip the door off the hinges, but it won't budge. We think that by our own strength or resolve we can get out. Or we think it is someone else's fault that we can't get out. It's not! You can't get out the door because you can't see the means—the key—that the Lord has provided for you. The key is to know the truth, and we know the truth primarily through his Word.

I want to ask a publishing company to make a Bible that says "Push to Exit" on the cover. Do you want to get out of the bondage you are in? You have the necessary truth that can set you free. Do you want to get free in your marriage struggles? Push to exit. Examine the truth of God's Word about the foundations of marriage, apply those truths, and you'll find the freedom you long for. Do you want to get free in your finances? Push to exit. Examine the truth of God's Word in regard to money and you'll find the freedom you long for. Do you want to get free in your temptations and your addictions? Push to exit. Do you want to get free from your past? Push to exit. Do you want to find redemption and forgiveness from all your sins? Push to exit.

It's actually not complicated. Earlier I said that God wants to be known. He is not trying to be hidden. He is truth. If we know him, then we know truth, and that's where we find freedom. Freedom and truth go hand in hand, and they are found in God's nature. Who is God? He is truth, absolutely and completely. His truth leads us to freedom.

The Challenge of Personal Obedience

As good as that sounds, there is still one more component to living out of our true identity as those free in Christ. God tells us clearly that we have to decide if we are going to take that path. "If you hold to my teaching, . . . *then* you will know the truth" (John 8:31–32, emphasis added). The last ingredient in this process is our willingness to submit to God's truth.

We must hold to his teaching and not our own. He is truth, and if we live according to that truth, we will find freedom. But we can still choose not to.

I'll be the first to admit that does not sound very freeing. It feels almost as if we are back to square one, living in bondage to the law. Not so. Think about this: no one is truly free in this world. People can say they are, but they're not. We are all bound by the laws of nature—I am not free from gravity. I am bound by the laws of the country I live in—I am not free to create anarchy. I am bound by the physical limitations of my body—I am not free to fly. I am bound by death—I am not free to live forever. So if the reality is that no one is truly free, then our task is to find the system of law to live in that affords us the greatest freedom—the freedom to live in the promised abundance of God.

Finding the right system, however, can be difficult because there are so many competing claims. Our world is like a big carnival with vendors barking at us about the wonders of their truth. With all the noise and people shouting, it can be confusing. Even so, go back to the basics. If the God who made us says that truth is found in him and by that truth we find freedom and life, then that's where I'm going to start. I'm going to be obedient to what he says. First John 1:8 reminds us, "If we claim to be without sin, we deceive ourselves and the truth is not in us." If we act as though we're our own god and that we know best, then we are deceiving ourselves. If we do that, we don't have the truth, and without the truth we'll never be free.

Let me give you an example. A little boy has terrible allergies. He desperately wants a pet, but his parents refuse to get him a dog or a cat because of the potential harm the allergies might cause. Then the boy's mother has a great idea—fish! She goes to the pet store, buys an exotic aquarium with numerous colorful fish, and takes it home to her son. He is thrilled. He finally has a pet, and lots of them. He and his mother sit in front of the aquarium. He names his fish. She is pleased. Problem solved—or so she thinks. She goes to the kitchen to make dinner. An hour later, the boy comes out of his room and slumps on the sofa. She asks if he is all right. He says, "I guess, but my fish really aren't that fun anymore." His mother is surprised. She asks, "Why not?" The boy says, "Well, at first it was great. I put them on my bed and they flopped around and played and had fun, but now they all just lay there."

Fish are created to live in a particular environment: water. They are free to live when they are in that environment. But a fish is not free to do whatever it wants. It cannot live on land. When a fish lives within the boundaries of water, it is free to be what God intended it to be. If we live as God intended, we will experience the abundance he promised because we are living within his will. We are living within the environment he created for us.

Here's the deal: God created the truth of his Word as the environment for us to live in. When we live within it, we are free to become the people God intended us to be. When we live within it, we submit to his will for us and can therefore experience the abundance he promised. Obviously, we can choose to ignore that environment. Many do. Yet where does that lead us? It leads us to the bondage of sin and darkness. Think for a moment about what the world would be like if we all obeyed God's Word. Think of all the social issues and problems that would disappear. Think of all the burdens that would be lifted. Life would not be perfect, because the world would still be fallen, but at the very least, we would not increase the burden of living in a fallen world by adding our own baggage.

It has been my privilege to know a number of people who have struggled with sexual brokenness and same-sex attraction. As hard as they tried to convince themselves that their behavior was okay, they never found freedom in it. It did not afford them the abundant life they thought it would. Bondage, not freedom, was the result. They never found freedom until they realized the love of God overwhelmed even their perceived need for the love of another. I have known people who insisted that drugs and alcohol were fine. What's the big deal if I take an occasional hit? As long as they deceived themselves and denied the truth, they lived in bondage. I have known people who lived solely for themselves, immersed in their own world, unfeeling, uncaring, unaware of the need to give, either personally or financially. You can deceive yourself all you want about your money, but as long as you live apart from God's truth, you'll be bound up by the very thing you think will make you free. The only way you can find freedom is by living according to God's truth about giving.

What Spiritual Freedom Is Not

Before I conclude this chapter, I need to address what may be the elephant in the room for you. When you started reading a chapter on finding freedom from burdens, you may have been expecting a formula that would get you out of your current circumstances or pain. That's not what spiritual freedom means. Spiritual freedom is not the absence of personal challenges. It does mean that even in my personal challenges, I am not bound by them in such a way that my identity changes. I may carry the burden of having lost my job, but the freedom given to me in Christ allows me to move forward without being defined by that loss. I am not what

I do; I am who Christ made me to be. So I'm not going to hang my head and believe I am worthless. That's bondage. Freedom comes in knowing the truth. The truth is that I am a child of the King.

I may carry the burden of physical infirmity or disease that limits my movements or activity, but the freedom given to me in Christ allows me to see my life as more than physical movement. God has infused my life with purpose and meaning as I serve the people who cross my path each day, regardless of my physical limitations. I am not going to believe I am useless simply because I am physically challenged. That's bondage. Freedom comes in knowing the truth. The truth is that my life has purpose. I am an instrument in the hands of God for his glory.

I may carry the burden of grief. It's painful and deep and raw, but the freedom given to me in Christ allows me to see my life as more than surviving loss. God has revealed to me that there is life after this one. My grief has been answered at the empty tomb. I am not going to allow my life to collapse on itself because I grieve. I am not going to pretend that my loved one is still here. That's bondage. I am going to look to the vision of heaven given to me in Scripture while waiting expectantly and hopefully for that day. Freedom comes in knowing the truth. The truth is that Jesus Christ has defeated death. It does not mean the pain is gone, but I'm not bound by it either. My freedom is in the hope of Christ and his resurrection.

More Than Physical Restrictions

Here's something else I have learned from my experiences in jails: freedom is more than your physical confines. When I went into the jail that day, I met a number of men who had

143

found the truth of God and his Word. As I spoke it and taught it, I could see the joy in their lives—they were experiencing freedom in a very profound way. In conversations with them afterward, I found men who knew the Lord deeply and who were experiencing the freedom of becoming the men God wants them to be. They were living a rich, abundant life in Christ, even in jail! It was inspiring to say the least.

Right now there are Christian men and women sitting in jail who are more free than you are. Somewhat shocking perhaps, but it's true. I came back to my church, looked at some of the people sitting in our pews weighed down by all their bags, and thought, *They are not in jail, but they are definitely not free.* That thought ought to be disturbing. Let me ask you: What is it that binds you? Is it binding you because you are denying what God says is true? If it is, and you want to be free, then you need to start doing what he says—not what you want—and live according to his truth. As you do that, you will live more and more within the environment he created for you, and you will find your identity as one set free in Christ, living out God's purpose for you in the world. Wow. That is true freedom. That is what we yearn for, and what deep relief it is when we find it. The chains fall off. The fear is gone. The door is open. Freedom!

In July of 2008, the world was astounded when a group of Colombian freedom fighters and American soldiers freed fifteen political hostages in Colombia, including Ingrid Betancourt, who had been kidnapped six years earlier while she was a Colombian candidate for president. Without a single shot being fired, the hostages were freed. The liberators' strategy was based on a ruse: Government agents had secretly infiltrated rebel ranks, and when the time was right, the agents used their new authority to gather the hostages onto helicopters and fly them to another location. When the choppers lifted off, the agents disarmed the rebels, pointed their guns at them, and told them to get down on the floor. Once secured, the agents turned to the stunned hostages and said, "We are the national military. You are free."[5]

Can you imagine what that must have been like? Can you imagine the joy and relief, having lived for more than six years in captivity and uncertainty, to hear the words, "You are free"? God tells us he came "to open eyes that are blind, to free captives from prison and to release from the dungeon those who sit in darkness" (Isa. 42:7). What joy we should have to hear those words, but when you've been bound up for so long, sometimes it's hard to believe you're free. Initially it seems impossible. Our first reaction is often: "Can this really be?" Yes, it can be. You are free. You are. God is truth. When you know him and live by his truth, you're free. Your freedom from the burdens and bags you carry has been ensured through the death of Christ. By his resurrection, those burdens and bags can be laid down.

Gently and lovingly, the crucified Christ helps lift those bags and burdens. He whispers in your ear, "Let me have them. Let go. You're free. These do not determine your identity. These do not determine your future. I have set you free to be who I made you to be." When we hear God's voice, the burden lifts. Our shoulders relax. Our hands unclench. No, the burdens don't magically disappear, but their weight is different. They no longer determine our identity. They no longer have such power over us. They no longer define our future. From that point on, we respond differently. We respond to God's Word with joyful obedience. We respond to God's Word as a gift that provides the boundaries from which we live, not as a burden we must carry.

If we want to know ourselves, we must know the God who made us. He has revealed that he is truth. His truth is what makes us free. We can choose to deny it, or we can choose to live within the boundaries of our true identity. The good news is that we are free. May we know the joy and wonder of those words, we who have been hostages unto ourselves far too long.

9

Why Do Others Always Let Me Down?

HOW GOD'S FAITHFULNESS RESTORES OUR CONFIDENCE

The one who calls you is faithful, and he will do it.

1 Thessalonians 5:24

By faithfulness we are collected and wound up into unity within ourselves, whereas we had been scattered abroad in multiplicity.

Saint Augustine

Jerry and Earlene. I'll never forget them.

My wife and I were leading a marriage retreat for a group from First Presbyterian Church in Colorado Springs, a church led by a dear friend and brother, Jim Singleton. The retreat was held at the Trail West Young Life Camp in Buena Vista, Colorado. It was mid-February and the "collegiate peaks"—Mounts Princeton, Yale, Columbia, Oxford, and Harvard—that rose toward the sky, covered in a glassy snow, were absolutely stunning. The valley below was equally majestic—a flat sea of gleaming ice that appeared to be endless. For a man who grew up in Texas and lives in the flatlands of Florida, it was a wondrous backdrop.

The first night we were there, my body clock was off. The altitude had given me a headache, and I was not sleeping well. I tossed and turned and finally decided it was time to get up. It was around six o'clock, and I was in serious need of coffee, so I stumbled in the dark to the main meeting room where we were told a coffeepot was always on.

As I entered the main room with its far wall of glass revealing the mountains, I saw this marvelous couple for the first time. I didn't notice them right away, but as I filled my cup I looked to my right, and there they were, sitting side by side in two folding chairs that were turned to face the mountains and the dawning light. My guess is that they were in their eighties, far and away the oldest couple on the retreat, but you would have been hard-pressed to find another couple with more energy and zest for life or more affection for each other.

Earlene wore a full-length velour robe with slippers that matched, and as she sat there, arm in arm with her husband, she appeared almost regal. He wore a plaid robe with beat-up slippers, but none of that mattered as his gaze alternated between the mountains and the face of his wife, softly illuminated by the first gentle rays of the sun.

I hated to disturb them, but they noticed my rustling and Jerry said, "Good morning, David. Come sit with us." Rarely had I received such an enthusiastic invitation at that hour, so I went over. My first question was, "What are you two doing up so early?"

Their answer provided further context for the richness of that first image I saw of them, arm in arm in those chairs. Jerry said, "Well, David, we've been married almost sixty years, and we discovered a long time ago that if we start our day together, giving thanks to the Lord and watching the sun rise, it keeps our hearts in the right place throughout the day. So each morning we get up and watch the sun rise as we talk to the Lord." With that, he looked at his wife, winked, and broke into a broad smile. I thought to myself, *Now there is a picture of what faithfulness looks like.*

Many times since then, I have thought about that image: two people, faithful to each other and to the Lord, watching the first hint of the sun rising over the mountains. It provides such a stark contrast to what is often experienced by many. Faithfulness is not the norm. We have grown accustomed to the opposite. We find few people who *are* faithful, who keep their promises, who do what they say, and who keep their word. So we develop a built-in mistrust of others. It's gotten to the point that we assume others will be unfaithful in some way—at least until proven otherwise.

I'll never forget the words of Murray Gossett, my high school youth pastor: "You can always tell the character of a man by the way he keeps the promises he makes in casual conversation." In other words, if you say you'll call, then call. If you say you'd like to have lunch, then make the plans and schedule the time. If you say you're going to come to an event, then show up. Today that character quality seems lost. *Faithfulness*, not just in marriage but also in many other situations, is not a word often used. Words like *betrayal*, *disloyalty*, and *infidelity* are more dominant.

Such behavior is expected. We can't count on the cable guy to show up when he says. We can't count on our sports heroes to actually act like heroes. We can't count on the price of gas or the value of the dollar. We can't count on our leaders to do what they say they're going to do. And because we're human beings, the reality is that we can't count fully on one another. We are always going to let each other down.

This lack of faithfulness is partly because of the way in which our culture views faith and God. We have gradually, but effectively, pushed God to the fringes. He is no longer viewed as the foundation for the social values and moral choices of our society. In the absence of a foundation that compels us to care for and love others, we digress to primarily caring about ourselves. Our motivation becomes doing what makes our lives better. The end justifies the means. If I have to go back on my word because I changed my mind, then so be it, because I am going to do what is best for me. I am going to do what is convenient for me. If I find that I'm not as interested in my wife after twenty years, then I'm going to go find someone new, because that's what's best for me. Those vows I took were a long time ago. If I have a huge real estate deal on the table but it means betraying one of my business partners, well that's just business. That's what's best for me. Culturally, we lack a foundation that upholds faithfulness, so we see it less.

Naturally, this has a tremendous negative impact on our identity. When we live with constant unfaithfulness, we start to identify ourselves as those who are abandoned. No one is faithful to us. We can't depend on anyone. We can't trust anyone. We become insular, keeping others at a safe relational distance in order to protect ourselves from betrayal. Our minds reason, "I won't let that happen to me again. I'll never allow someone to hurt me that way." While that may be true, we are also keeping away the very things that make life meaningful: love, community, shared experiences, support, and accountability. Our identities melt into fear, mistrust, and a deep-seated belief that we are not worthy of another's fidelity.

If we believe that no one is faithful—not even God—the consequences multiply. Our identity becomes one of absolute and utter control. We build carefully constructed walls, spending enormous emotional and mental energy to ensure their strength and maintenance. We become obsessive and compulsive about everything that happens in our lives because of our root belief that everyone will eventually betray us. It's *every man for himself*, so we build up the machinery of our lives to survive in such a world. If we can't trust anyone—and we eliminate God from that equation too—then the only person we can trust is ourselves.

I don't know about you, but if the only person I can count on is me, I am in bad shape. Why? I know I'm not trustworthy. I make mistakes all the time. My desires are not pure. My heart is not always in the right place. My motives are often questionable. If I depend on me, I usually make a mess of it. I don't believe that's who we actually want to be. That's not the identity we want to live out of, but we honestly don't know any other way. We think, in light of the evidence, this is who we are—who we must be—in order to survive. Even so, we still crave faithfulness. If we find a glimmer of it, we cling to it like it's the Hope Diamond. We yearn for it, but our foundational belief is that we won't find it.

We Crave Faithfulness

In the spring of 1990, with my last year of seminary looming and both of us working, my wife and I went from being a one-car family to a two-car family. I purchased a slightly used red Honda Civic Hatchback for $7,700, and it remains the best car I've ever had. It took me from seminary in Texas to my first job in Tennessee. It took me with great haste to the hospital when Leigh went into labor with our first child. It took me from Charlotte, North Carolina, back to Chattanooga in a driving snowstorm—a six-hour trip that became a twelve-hour nightmare. It was never in an accident, never broke down, never failed to start, and never had a flat tire. That car was utterly dependable.

Perhaps the greatest example of this dependability was a spring night in 1993 when Leigh and I had gone out to see a movie. As we sat in the theater, we heard a thunderstorm popping outside, but we didn't think much of it. When it was time to go, we ran through the rain and started home, again not really thinking about the amount of rain that had been falling. As we turned onto the main road home, we were met by a wall of water coming right at us. It was a flash flood. If you have never been in one, they are *incredibly* scary. Water rushed down the road as if it was a river.

Cars stalled or drifted with the water into roadside ditches. People were abandoning their cars, struggling through waist-high water to get to higher ground. All I could think about was not stalling my engine. The water was now coming over the hood of my car. I didn't think my little Honda was going to make it, but it did. To this day, I don't know why my engine never stalled, but we kept moving just enough to make it to the next cross street, outperforming four-wheel drive vehicles, and got to higher ground and eventually back home. I loved that car because not once did it let me down.

We love things we can depend on, don't we? We love things that are faithful. It's why we love our pets, our postal carriers, and Yellowstone Park. One of the biggest tourist attractions in our country is not Old Inconsistent but Old Faithful. Since being discovered in 1870, that geyser has erupted every 35 to 120 minutes for a duration of 90 seconds to 5 minutes. It is not the biggest geyser in the nation nor the biggest one in Yellowstone Park, so why do people come to see it? They come because they can depend on it to erupt. They know that when they go, they won't be let down. People go because they are drawn to things that are faithful. We crave it. We need it.

We desperately want to find something—someone—in whom we can put our complete trust and faith. We want to know they are going to do what they say, that they will never let us down. Thankfully, as 1 Thessalonians 5:24 affirms, we have just that person. God is that person. God *is faithful*. Paul says God is going to do the things he has promised to do. We can trust that. If we're honest, part of us thinks, *What a relief*, but there is another part of us that wonders, *Can I believe that?*

Wrestling with God

We read the Scriptures and hear the promises and do the Bible studies and listen to the sermons, and we want to believe it's true. We desperately want to believe that God is faithful. But is he? We want to stop living out of a fearful identity that trusts no one, but do we dare believe this is true? I'm not sure we do. While we want to believe it, we struggle with evidence that appears to be to the contrary. Was God faithful when he allowed a hurricane to bear down on southern Louisiana, destroying the lives of thousands—many of whom loved the Lord and were faithful to him—leaving them for months without proper shelter or nutrition? Was God faithful to a mother who faithfully came to church and openly professed her faith in the Lord when her five-year-old daughter was ejected and killed in a car accident even though she was belted in? In this economy, has God been faithful to the many who love him and have given their lives to him even as their jobs are threatened or lost, their income cut, or their savings diminished? Such events leave us wondering, *God, I want to believe you're faithful, but are you?*

Doubt about God's faithfulness is actually what causes many people to abandon their faith altogether. Something happens and they decide, *Well, I'm done with God. He didn't hold up his end.* It is also one of the biggest obstacles people face when considering faith in God. They think, *God says he's faithful, but I see evidence to the contrary, so I'm not sure if I can believe it's true. Therefore I won't commit.* As we wrestle with this, the voices of our culture chime in and prey upon our fears. We are led to believe that faith in God is untenable, believable only by those without the intellectual acuity to think clearly. We are led to believe that the only god who exists is the one who lives within us: the god of self. So we come full circle, right back to having no one else to depend on but ourselves.

So which is it? Is God faithful, or must we depend on ourselves? Is it possible that we can know God's nature so deeply that we can say with Job, "The LORD gave, and the LORD hath taken away; blessed be the name of the LORD" (Job 1:21 KJV)? Or is God unfaithful, or perhaps worse, unable to keep the promises he has made? If we find our circumstances painful and overwhelming, can God really be trusted and depended on, or should we start looking for something else in life?

The Fidelity of God

I want to examine these questions in light of 1 Thessalonians 5:23–24. This is a letter written by Paul to the church in Thessalonica, a church that was struggling with some of the same issues. Christians were having serious doubts about God's faithfulness because they had seen the viciousness of the people who threatened Paul and ran him out of town. They had seen the raw conflict between Jews and Christians—lives threatened and families torn apart. They had heard all the same promises that we have heard, and they naturally wondered, "With all these things happening, is this really worth it? If we stake our lives on this faith, will God really be faithful?" They struggled with it, and we struggle with it, which is why it is important for us to look at Paul's words and the context of this truth to see what God reveals about his faithfulness.

Paul's primary assertion is that God is faithful in his nature. Faithfulness is part of the perfection of his being. Over and over again, we are reminded of this in Scripture.

He is the faithful God. (Deut. 7:9)

[God] is faithful in all he does. (Ps. 33:4)

His faithfulness continues through all generations. (Ps. 100:5)

For in perfect faithfulness you have done wonderful things. (Isa. 25:1)

God is faithful. (1 Cor. 1:9)

The one who calls you is faithful. (1 Thess. 5:24)

The Lord is faithful. (2 Thess. 3:3)

There before me was a white horse, whose rider is called Faithful and True. (Rev. 19:11)

New Testament, Old Testament—no matter the context or circumstance—in all things God is revealed as faithful.

God's eternal faithfulness also reveals our lack of faith. He is faithful, and our nature is not. Hosea 2:2 says we are adulterous and unfaithful. 2 Timothy 2:13 says, "If we are faithless, he remains faithful." We know it's true. You and I are never going to be completely faithful to anything, period, which is why it is all the more important for us to find someone who is.

God is faithful, and you actually depend on this more than you realize. If we believe God is the Creator, then we must also agree that he sustains that creation. He is sovereign over that creation. When you get up each morning, you do not fear that the sun will not rise, that night will never yield to day. You depend on God's faithfulness to do that. You go to sleep at night believing that God will wake you in the morning. You do not fret and worry that spring will somehow not follow winter. You do not wonder if the grass will again wake to a fresh green or that the flowers, long dormant, will bloom again. He has told us he is faithful, and, given the rhythms and cycles of what he has made, we see that he is. We believe it and depend on it more than we even realize.

The Limits and Purpose of God's Faithfulness

In understanding God's faithfulness, we must be careful not to make assumptions as to its scope. God is faithful only to who he is. In other words, he can only be faithful to his plan and purpose. He cannot be faithful to evil. He cannot be faithful to something that contradicts himself. God will always be faithful to his attributes and nothing else. Thus it is not blanket faithfulness, but faithfulness within the confines of his nature. Psalm 33:10–11 reminds us, "The LORD foils the plans of the nations; he thwarts the purposes of the peoples.

But the plans of the LORD stand firm forever, the purposes of his heart through all generations."

The Lord is faithful to what's in his heart, what's in his nature. He is not going to be faithful to your plan or my plan, to your choices or my choices. He is going to be faithful only to his purpose. In 1 Thessalonians 5:23, Paul reminds us of what that is. "May God himself, the God of peace, sanctify you through and through. May your whole spirit, soul and body be kept blameless at the coming of our Lord Jesus Christ." What is God's purpose? His purpose is to save and sanctify us. That's the plan to which he is going to be faithful.

Correspondingly, the Lord will not be faithful to what he has not promised. This is where we get confused at times. He did not promise that you will never be sick and never know pain, so if you are sick or in pain, it does not mean God is not faithful. He did not promise that your marriage will be perfect or that all your relationships will be fulfilling, so if your marriage fails or your friend betrays you, that does not mean God is not faithful. He did not promise that you will have children or that your children will live a certain number of years, so as hard as it is, if you have a miscarriage or are unable to get pregnant or if your child is taken from you in some way—physically, emotionally, or spiritually—it does not mean God is not faithful. He did not promise a problem-free world; in fact, he promised the opposite. Jesus said, "In this world you will have trouble" (John 16:33). Paul writes in 1 Peter 4:12, "Do not be surprised at the painful test you are suffering" (GNT).

God has not promised us a trouble-free life, but he has assured us of some very important things. He has promised us his nature as a God of peace. He has promised us his presence through which we find peace in the knowledge that no matter what happens, he is at work. He has promised that he will sanctify and save the entirety of our being—spirit, soul, and body—working all things together for good.

Paul writes in Romans 8:28, "And we know that in all things God works for the good of those who love him, who have been called according to his purpose." In Genesis 50:20, after all that Joseph had been through, he said, "You intended to harm me, but God intended it for good to accomplish what is now being done, the saving of many lives." God promises us that he is faithful to his plan and purpose, even when our external issues or circumstances may look destructive or unfair. God can still work them out for good, for the saving of many lives!

What God has promised is his faithful presence—he will never leave us or abandon us. That is revealed most completely in the coming of Jesus Christ. God came to be with us in Christ. He kept his promise. He is faithful.

Our Struggle with Time

One of the biggest challenges we have to overcome in understanding God's faithfulness is its relationship to time. As human beings, we are bound by time and space. Consequently, we tend to put those same limitations on God, but he exists outside of time and space. We are physical and finite. God is spirit and infinite. He is not like us in his being, so he is not bound by the same things that constrain us. Therefore God's faithfulness is not determined by timing.

First Thessalonians 5:24 says, "The one who calls you is faithful, and he will do it." Paul tells the people of God's faithfulness, but then he reminds them that faithfulness is an act that will take place in the future. It *will* happen. That word denotes time, so we need to recall God's view of time: "A thousand years in your sight are like a day that has just gone by" (Ps. 90:4). God exists outside of our human dimensions, which we don't understand. We want to keep parameters of time and immediacy on God's faithfulness, but he does not work according to our time. He works in his time.

Even knowing that, we still try to use time as a measurement of God's faithfulness. We lose our job and don't get another one for an extended period of time, so we start to doubt whether God is faithful. We get sick and linger in that illness. God does not heal us, so we start to question his faithfulness. When God does not act according to our time, we tend to get angry or bitter and say he is not faithful. We falsely believe that God is not keeping up his end of the bargain, but that entire assessment is based on our time or timing. Using that as a measurement is false.

Time is not what defines his faithfulness. God is never late, but neither is he hurried. He will always act in his time. God was faithful to the Israelites to redeem them from their bondage, but their slavery lasted more than four hundred years. God was faithful to bring them into the Promised Land, but they were still in the desert for forty years. God was faithful in sending the Messiah, but it was five hundred years after the last prophetic voice announced his coming. God was faithful to Lazarus, Mary, and Martha, even though Lazarus actually died before Jesus arrived. Yes, God *will* do it, but we cannot define his faithfulness according to the hands on our watch or according to our timing. We don't have the full picture; only God does. So we trust in what God has revealed, and we build our lives around the bedrock of his faithfulness.

More than Words and Platitudes

As you are reading through this chapter, you may be tempted right here to say, "That's just psychological banter to make us feel better." And that's exactly what our culture wants us to believe. There is one trump card they are missing, however—one element that must be considered as the lynchpin of all I have said. These are not mere words or a collection of sweet-sounding platitudes. We know this because of one thing: the cross of Jesus Christ.

It is at the cross of Jesus where God demonstrates, fully and completely, the fullness of his faithfulness, for there he answered our pains by taking them on himself. God answered our suffering by his own suffering. He answered our humiliation by being humiliated. He answered what threatens our life by defeating death. Thus if we accept that on the third day they could not find the body of Jesus and that he rose, then God *is* faithful to what he has promised: this life is not all there is, so his main concern is our eternal life—our salvation and sanctification.

God has never promised us comfort, but he has promised to be faithful in building our Christlike character. He has never promised us the absence of circumstantial chaos, but he has promised us his presence and his peace. He has not promised that we will never experience injustice or tragedy, but he has promised us that those things will never be the final word, because the final Word has been given once and for all in Jesus.

Impacting Our Identity

As we look at this world and all that seems to betray us, as we struggle in our identity to believe that we are more than merely a lost, abandoned soul unworthy of fidelity, who is God? God is faithful. He has done exactly what he promised. He has been faithful to his nature as a holy, loving God. Thus when we take this to heart, our identity changes. We no longer need the meticulously crafted walls that we have constructed in order to protect ourselves from betrayal. We no longer need to insulate ourselves from a world that scares us. We no longer need to define ourselves as abandoned or betrayed.

This is not going to happen instantly, but the more we internalize the faithfulness of God revealed in Jesus Christ, the more confidence we will gain in approaching our world. I am not suggesting that we blindly put ourselves in situations where we can be taken advantage of. I am not suggesting that we not use our head. I *am* suggesting that we can learn to live from an identity born out of confidence in God's faithfulness, not fear of betrayal. We can live out of an identity grounded in the love of the Father, not an identity scarred by love withheld. When we live out of that identity, our spirit and our heart become open to what God may have for us. We can be open to the possibility of being loved and supported and cared for. We can stop being afraid of commitment, instead embracing it because ultimately we are grounded in the unyielding commitment of the Father. Over time this will make each of us a different person—a new person—because of an identity in which we know we are worthy of faithfulness. We are not abandoned. We are loved, now and eternally.

From there, we move on to bear witness to God's faithfulness in the world, living out our identity as those who are faithful. Contrary to the way the world works, we do what we say. Our yes means yes and our no means no. We keep our promises. We are faithful in our marriages. We are dependable in our friendships. If God is faithful in his nature and he comes to live in us through Christ, then we have the inherent capacity to live faithfully and obediently to him, being used by God as his instruments and agents in the world. We can live faithfully in our relationships with others because we see how faithful God is to us. We can model for others what dependability and trustworthiness look like because we have learned them from the Father.

We live in uncertain times. Natural disasters have taken thousands of lives and inflicted tremendous suffering on thousands more. We continue to wonder about our economy and what is happening to our jobs and our nest eggs. We anxiously listen to ongoing reports of a roiling Middle East. It is as unsettling a time as any in recent memory. Yet as I have struggled with that, I find myself repeating the same thing over and over to those who come to see me with concerns about their lives and their world: we may not know what's happening or why, but we trust in the one who does. God is faithful, and he is at work to bring about his plan and purpose. Take confidence and peace in that.

Just today I had a man in my office weeping over issues related to his son and another man weeping over struggles in his marriage. Neither could fathom what was happening or why his loved one had chosen to make certain decisions. Both struggled to find God in the messiness and pain of their lives. I found myself saying it yet again: I know it's hard right now, but God is faithful. Trust God. Live out of that confidence.

10

Why Do I Feel So Bad about Myself?

HOW GOD'S LOVE TRANSFORMS OUR SELF-IMAGE

And now these three remain: faith, hope and love. But the greatest of these is love.

1 Corinthians 13:13

The Christian does not think God will love us because we are good, but that God will make us good because He loves us.

C. S. Lewis

I was busy backstage when I saw him for the first time. I was leading a youth conference at Jekyll Island, Georgia, and was planning details for the evening program. One part was a testimony by a young man named Joel. Someone on the staff had heard his testimony months earlier and invited him to speak, but I had never met him.

He wore a plaid button-down shirt, jeans, flip-flops, and a baseball hat. His eyes were deeply expressive, sharp, and clear. When he looked at you, it was as if he saw your heart. Honestly, it felt intimidating.

While he looked at me, I found it hard to look at him. My difficulty was not because of his piercing eyes but because he had no hair, no eyelids, no ears, and no lips. His rebuilt nose breathed oxygen into his body—a body that had been burned over 90 percent of its surface ten years earlier. The details of the accident were of no consequence in light of their result: a body so badly burned, so grossly disfigured that he barely resembled a human being.

It was hard not to stare, but he acted as if everything was perfectly normal. He did not seem the least bit self-conscious but instead was confident, poised, and calm. He had endured hundreds of hours of plastic surgeries and skin grafts, physical rehabilitation, painful bandaging, the formation of scar tissue, and constant infections that threatened his life, yet here he was, ready to speak to 1,500 high school students.

Since I was going to introduce him, I asked questions about his story, trying to wrap my mind around what I should say. As we chatted, I discovered a young man who was warm, engaging, bright, funny, self-effacing, and articulate. And Joel loved Jesus. My goodness, did he ever love Jesus.

He talked about the agony of his recovery, how he came to know the Lord, how the love of Jesus had filled his life, and how he had learned that his beauty was defined by how God saw him, not how the world saw him. That was his testimony. His words were often accompanied by a warm, wide smile as he thought about all that God had done in his life.

I found it almost too much to believe. How does someone burned over 90 percent of his body ever smile about anything, much less act as if he is the most blessed man on the planet— all at the age of eighteen? Here's what I found amazing: in a twenty-minute conversation, I went from feeling shocked by his physical appearance to feeling drawn to this young man's heart and life. In a word, Joel was *attractive*.

Here's the other thing: when Joel spoke to those 1,500 students, they were absolutely mesmerized. They couldn't understand it either. When he finished, they erupted in thunderous applause. But Joel was not done impacting our camp. He didn't leave, and over the next two days he participated in camp activities. He went to the beach. He played volleyball and Ultimate Frisbee. As he did, he was a rock star. He had students following him all the time, and not just the male students. The female students surrounded him everywhere he went.

By worldly standards, this young man was ugly and disfigured. He had none of the exterior *look* that defines cool for his generation, and yet there he was, acting like the Pied Piper. How was such a thing possible? It became quickly apparent to all of us: love. His identity had been transformed, presently and eternally, by one simple truth: God loves him. God's love is so powerful that he no longer views himself through the eyes of the world but through the eyes of God. And because he sees himself that way, the beauty of God's love pours out of him so that others see him exactly that way: he is beautiful.

I don't know about you, but I want to know that love. I want to know God's love so deeply and so surely that it changes my identity at my core. We all want that, but we seem hopelessly unable to grasp it.

Instead, we wallow in a sea of comparison, feeling lousy about ourselves because we don't stack up to the pictures in the magazines or the co-workers in our office or the people we read about in the paper. We buy into a message that says our identity is measured by who we're with, how we look, and how much we make. Regardless of our age, we stumble into pursuing those things in order to validate a false sense of self. As soon as that pursuit fails, we are crushed by despair, believing we're unworthy. Our self-esteem plummets.

Unfortunately, in the absence of truth we accept those false measurements as valid. We think they *are* the true measure. The faulty measurements become our identity. If that's what we struggle with, then our task is to discover what Joel knew deeply—we need to understand God's love. We need to move it from our heads to our hearts so it transforms our identity.

The Ultimate Moral Hazard

While that sounds easy on one level, it's not. It's not easy because of the way our culture approaches and defines love itself. Love has lost its true meaning, and we need to get it back. The word *love* is so overused and misused that it scarcely resembles the God-created version.

Several years ago, as our Congress was debating the pros and cons of a $700 billion bailout package to try to avert an economic catastrophe, I heard a phrase being repeated that I had not heard before. It was used by both Alan Greenspan and Ben Bernanke on more than one occasion as they testified before a congressional finance committee. The term was this: *moral hazard.*

On the surface, that sounds like something you want to avoid. It sounds to me much like the new restaurant that has opened in my neighborhood that serves ridiculously delicious, fat-laden, heart-attack-provoking hamburgers that tempt me on a daily basis. I drive by it and say, "Well, there's a moral hazard." On further investigation, however, I found that is not what it means.

In the case of our financial fortunes, the term *moral hazard* actually dates back hundreds of years, primarily in France. The concept of a moral hazard means this: if you reduce the risk of something too far, then you unwittingly expose people to making poor moral choices. For example, if I take all the risk out of an unethical business deal for you, promising you absolute confidentiality, that no one will ever know, and assuring you that even if discovered, it could never be traced back to you, then I am responsible for creating a moral hazard in your life. By taking away the risk, I am creating a higher likelihood that you will make a poor moral choice. In the case of our financial markets, mortgages became so easy and appeared to carry such little risk that financial institutions created a moral hazard for many families. They made poor choices about mortgages they could not afford because of how easy the banks had made it to obtain them.

If there is no risk to us, we are far more prone to do something stupid. Reducing the magnitude of something, making it appear less weighty than it is, will lead us to decisions that otherwise we would not make. I really like the term *moral hazard* because I have finally found something that I think describes what has happened to our culture—even to our church—in regard to our spiritual understanding of *love*.

Love is a word that is so overused and so poorly used that it no longer possesses any actual meaning. One person may use it to mean one thing, but it can have a totally different meaning for someone else. There's no substance to it. It reminds me of what happens in the summers in Tennessee when all the cicadas come out at night. They land on various things and make a lot of noise, but eventually they shed their skin. The next morning you may see a cicada sitting on a table outside, but when you shoo it away, you find it is only an empty shell.

The word *love* today is an empty shell. On the outside, it sounds like it has meaning, but it is empty. The life has gone out of it insofar as what God originally intended for us to know. As we understand *love* today, it has become a moral hazard. We have reduced its meaning to something so little, something that requires no effort, risk, or sacrifice, that we are tempted to make it only for us and about us. And that false understanding becomes dangerous. It's a moral hazard.

If love is only about us and what is easy and pleasurable for us, then that is a fundamental misunderstanding of God's essential nature. Love is defined today as a mushy, sappy, all-inclusive, self-driven wonder drug that becomes the panacea for the problems of the world. We say over and over again, "If people would just love each other, then it would all be okay." Well would it? If love is reduced to this very base understanding, would it be okay or would it be a moral hazard?

The summer of 1967 was better known as the "Summer of Love." I was four at the time, so I was not too caught up in it, but from what I have read, it was a time ripe with the tensions of war, racism, and politics. As a result, a group of people collectively known as *hippies* began to live according to an ideology of love not hate, peace not war. Their slogan was *free love*, and an event was planned in upstate New York to show the world what it was like to truly live in love.

That movement culminated in the summer of 1969 at Woodstock, New York, where the expected 100,000 people turned into a crowd of 1.5 million, and what was intended to be a witness of love became a horrific display of our most vile nature. People went berserk. Peter Townsend, a member of a band called the Who, which played at the event, said this: "What was going on off the stage was just beyond comprehension—stretchers and dead bodies, people throwing up, people on drug trips—I thought the whole of America had gone mad."[1]

Bill Bright writes, "What was supposed to be a monument to free love and brotherhood was actually a hedonistic mess resulting in total chaos; selfishness and a disregard for others reigned."[2] Perhaps we do not see it lived out with such shocking evidence today, but we are trapped in the same philosophy. The word *love* has become so stripped of its essential nature that it is not a blessing but a moral hazard that promotes choices that lead us away from God and toward the worship of self. Love is a fairy tale, love is free, love is about me; therefore we take risks and make choices that threaten the very life God has for us.

The implications of this affect not only our culture but also Christ's church. In many denominations, including my own, the church has lost her relevance in the world because God's love has become like everyone else's. We do whatever we want because that's what love means: letting people do whatever makes them happy. And if personal happiness is our goal, it will never be enough. We'll remain in the same trap of personal comparison. There will always be someone more talented, more attractive, and more gifted, and we'll wallow in the emptiness of pursuing what is false. We're empty, and we need God's love to save us.

Reclaiming a True Understanding of God's Love

Who we are, our true identity, is not found in the comparisons or measurements of this world but in the love of God. When we fully grasp his divine nature—that God is love—and allow that love to fill us, then we truly know who we are. Our identity is secure, just as Joel discovered. Our search for this understanding naturally brings me to one of the most well-known texts in all of Scripture—Paul's famous love chapter: 1 Corinthians 13. I have heard this read countless times at weddings, and of course my wife often repeats it to friends when describing the many ways in which I love and care for her. (If you truly believe that, then you are not as wise as I assumed!)

What we often do not understand in exploring this text is the striking similarity of Corinth to the way our culture understands love today. Corinth was a very prosperous city that was growing rapidly and thriving economically. In the midst of all that prosperity, it became known for rampant sexual immorality. The temple of Aphrodite, the goddess of love, was perched high above the city, celebrating the darkness of the city below. The Corinthians' understanding of love had fallen so far as to be almost solely understood in relationship to sex. Sound familiar? It was so bad that a new word was added to the vernacular of the time: casual sexual relations was called *Corinthianizing*.

Our assumptions about the sweet, sappy nature of Paul's discourse on love could not be further from the truth. When Paul wrote those words, he was not imagining them being romantically recited at weddings. He was engaged in a battle for the soul of a city. Love was completely misunderstood. They didn't know what godly love was. Love cost nothing. Love meant nothing. Love had become a moral hazard to God's people, and Paul was desperate to change that course. Consequently, he taught them about marriage, idolatry, and proper worship. He reminded them of Israel's failures in the past and then affirmed them for the many gifts they had as a body.

Then he came to the core of his argument. None of that, he said, would make one iota of difference if they didn't understand one thing: the true nature of love. I can't say this more bluntly: we are in the same boat. If we, as Christians and as a culture, don't understand what love really is and what it means for us, then we are headed for the same vile pit that the city of Corinth found itself in during the time of Paul. In fact, we may already be on the way. For far too long we have allowed a culturally shaped version of love to inform our identity and our behavior, to define what we believe to be true about ourselves. No more! It is a lie from the pit of hell, and we need to examine the depths of Paul's words to reclaim our true identity as the beloved sons and daughters of the living God!

Discovering God's True Nature

It's important to begin with an accurate definition of the word, according to God's Word. What is love, really? Beginning in 1 Corinthians 13:4, Paul provides the answer, and he does so in a way that is rarely seen. Love is a person. Love is an action. Contrary to popular belief, love is not a state of being. In this text, it's not a verb; it's a noun, personified by Paul: Love is patient, kind, not envious or boastful, not proud or rude or self-seeking, but gentle and forgiving and truthful. It protects and trusts and hopes. *Love is countercultural.* It does not operate the way the world operates.

Love, in its biblical sense, is counterintuitive. Why? Because while we want to be self-centered, love is not; while we want to do what we desire regardless of others, love does not allow it; while we want to hoard material things for ourselves, love wants to give. Love is sacrifice. Love is humility. Love is putting yourself last. Now test yourself in this. Put your name in the text and see how you do. David is patient. Gong. David is kind. Gong. David does not envy or boast. Nope. Gong. I have to stop. Do you see? Love is hard. Love is not about me or what I want; it's about something that I give—something that I offer—something that I am not normally prone to do. I'm wired to do for me, not to do for others.

Here's the question: If I can't put my name in there and you can't put your name in there, then what name belongs there? One name, and only one: the name of the Lord. Yahweh. Jehovah. Elohim. The only name that fits is that name that "is above every name, that at the name of Jesus every knee should bow, in heaven and on earth and under the earth, and every tongue acknowledge that Jesus Christ is Lord, to the glory of God the Father" (Phil. 2:9–11). The wonder of Paul's words in 1 Corinthians 13 is born through the way he personifies them. They are a personification of God, revealed through his Son and our Savior, Jesus Christ. When you understand that, the text explodes!

The God of the universe, the God of creation, the God who made you and me is defined by an element of his nature that sets us free. *God is love.* The only name that works there is God's name, and we know God best through his Son, Jesus. Jesus is patient with us. Jesus is kind. Jesus is not proud. He doesn't boast or envy. He always protects and always trusts and always gives hope. When we put it like that, we suddenly realize what God is doing in the text. It is not merely a random personification, but Paul has a distinct person in mind—and that person is the one he witnessed in Jesus Christ. That's who *love* is. First John 4:8 says, "Whoever does not love does not know God, because *God is love*" (emphasis added).

Love and Pain

Who is God really? God is love, and Paul describes how God has treated us in Christ with his love—patiently and kindly and humbly and sacrificially. He's not love in the way we may think he is or perhaps even the way we want him to be, where being loved by him means we can do whatever we want, where love is just about me and my happiness. God is not love in a way that means he is supposed to meet all of our needs and answer all of our prayers in exactly the way we want. God's love does not mean he is a cosmic vending machine.

God wants so much more for each of us than that because he loves us. First John 3:16 says, "This is how we know what love is: Jesus Christ laid down his life for us." That's what love is, and that's who love is. Love is not easy. Love is hard, and it demands our investment, our time, and our heart. To love someone is to risk, to care, and to engage. Love is pure joy and sometimes pleasure, but be assured, love also hurts, and that is often the dynamic we miss.

On her blog, *A Holy Experience*, Ann Voskamp relates an experience with love that hurts. She is grieving that her last baby is growing up. The little girl sees her mother's tears and asks, "You sad, Mama?"

> The words ache in my throat. . . . "I just never want to be done with babies . . . Wonders like you." . . .
>
> "You always want a real baby that cries?"
>
> Her little string of words yank. Baby dolls like hers, stuffed and stitched and painted, can be rocked and bundled close and sang to. Wondered over. But they're not real babies. Just gilded.
>
> I've figured her words. Real babies are real because they feel this world's real ache . . . like we all do. It's part of the coming here. She doesn't know it, but she's asking me if I know that *real love embraces pain, gathers up the sadness, gently rocks the howling places.*
>
> Her child words startle with Kingdom truth: *Love's only tenderly real if it knows the taste of tears. I want gilded time,*

*goldenly stilled, wrapped close and held tight. But that's not
real. What's real, hurts.*

Yes, child, so you know it: *lament threads through real
love.*[3]

Yes, real love. That's what we want. That's *who* we want.
Not easy love, but love that matters—love that invests and
cares and hurts with us. We want love that enters our pain,
feels our hurt, and rocks us gently until we sleep. We want love
that sees through our failures and mistakes and loves us all the
same. When we find such love, we are transformed. That's the
kind of love that changes us. Love that demands nothing and
allows me to do whatever I want will never transform who I
am or how I view the world. Real love does. God's love does.

A Love That Transforms Us

That's what God reveals. Real love. God gave himself up for
you. Has anyone ever done that for you? Has anyone ever died
for you so that you could live? In order to fully understand
this, take some time to study the Gospel texts on the last
week of Jesus's life, his suffering and dying. Do some work
on the historicity of the cross. Your life will never be the
same. Paul writes of that work in 2 Corinthians 5:21, "God
made him who had no sin to be sin for us, so that in him we
might become the righteousness of God."

Jesus was innocent. He did nothing wrong, yet his love for
us was so deep that he received the punishment we deserved
in order that we could be reconciled back to the Father's love.
That should change us. That should change our churches,
our communities, and our world. But that's not happening,
is it? You know why? We don't know what love is. We have
so effectively moved God to the edges that we're not grasping

174

his love for us or his call for us to love others. When churches adapt to the culture in such a way that they lose the meaning of God's love, those churches then change and transform nothing. They teach and distribute the same kind of self-directed syrup that our culture is heaping on us, and that recipe fails. It changes no one.

I came across a book not long ago written by Will Blythe. It was not a book about faith or God but about basketball. Given my own interest in that subject, I dove in expecting one thing but suddenly found him describing his boredom with the church. He says:

> I had been drowsy all those years because church was boring. The [church] has reduced God from a voice out of the whirlwind to a gentle breeze whispering through the parking lot, from an awesome mystery into a civics lesson, from the power and the glory to the friendly and concerned. That's if He's around at all. Thus, church attendance was an exercise in being good, in should and shouldn't. You rarely encountered joy or terror. You were rarely ever possessed by the spirit. This was religion as a Rotary Club meeting . . . as a dead magnet with no power to attract, offering comfort and duty and nostalgia in the place of the shock and disorientation of genuine spiritual feeling. Why have I been a latecomer to the ball, forced to substitute metaphor for event, interpretation for prophecy, question for answer?[4]

Ouch. Our false idea of love has infected even our churches, and that infection has had consequences. Where is a love that transforms and changes us? Where is a love that helps us see and understand ourselves as we truly are in God's eyes? Where is the shock and disorientation of God's love? It's gone because we don't understand it.

God's love should shock us. The cross does not shock? We should be stunned by the magnitude of such suffering and sacrifice; we should be leveled by the knowledge that it was done for us; we should be completely disoriented by what it means. And from that moment on, nothing and no one can ever be the same. We are loved. *We* are loved. We are *loved*. We are loved *by God*. Drink that in. Linger there. Let it settle in your heart. We should be wholly disoriented because nothing in our world works that way. No one acts that way. No one loves any of us that way.

Disoriented for Change

If we grasp the stunning nature of God's love, where does that leave us? Having found real love, we stagger shocked and disoriented to the doorway of true life. So what do we do? That's what Paul is trying to get the Corinthian church to understand. Love becomes a noun. Love becomes enacted. What do we do? *We receive God's love, we love God back, and we love others.* If God's true love dwells in us, then this is our true nature. Jesus says, "Love the Lord your God with all your heart and with all your soul and with all your mind and with all your strength. . . . [and] love your neighbor as yourself" (Mark 12:30–31).

Perhaps we miss the implication of that verse. It implies that we first love ourselves. If you do not know you are loved, then it is impossible to love others unconditionally in the manner of Christ. Why? You will always be manipulating others to get what you don't have. Because our human nature is always driven by self, if I don't know I am loved by God, if my cup of love is not full, then either consciously or unconsciously, my interactions with you will be based on getting that cup filled. I am going to work hard to get what I need. I'll do things for you. I'll treat you well. I'll give and I'll sacrifice, but it will all be done with a hope and an expectation that you are going to love me back. I know we'll never love perfectly in this life, but I do believe we can change and grow in our ability to love by learning to receive God's love.

Don't misunderstand: we love ourselves not out of pride or selfish arrogance but through the humble understanding of God's sacrifice. We love ourselves because we know what we have been rescued from, and the lengths to which God was willing to go to accomplish that saving work. Zephaniah 3:17 is one of my favorite verses because it helps me internalize how much God loves me. The prophet writes, "[God] will take great delight in you; in his love he will no longer rebuke you, but will rejoice over you with singing."

When you woke up this morning, was your first waking thought, "God is so delighted with me today"? I bet it wasn't. It's not usually mine either. That's what I mean when I say God's love disorients us. It catches us off guard. God *is* delighted with you. God delights *in* you. In fact, he is so delighted that it makes him want to sing. I know. It's shocking, but it's true. When I let that truth wash over me, it changes me. The disorientation of God's wondrous love changes how I see myself.

When I was in my early twenties and struggling with the panic disorder I described earlier, I felt worthless and unloved. I felt like a broken, discarded instrument. What changed me was my discovery of God's love. Did I have those burdens? Yes, I did. But God's view of me was one of support, comfort, and love. Even in my weakened state, God delighted in my life. God saw my pain and my hurt, and as I struggled, he sang over me. And I finally started to hear the words. "David, you are loved. I know you wish you didn't have to deal with this. I know you feel broken and useless, but I am at work because I love you. I have redeemed your life. I have defeated this panic disorder, and I am delighted with you, my son, my precious, precious son." That was the song. Those were the lyrics to the song that God sang over me, and those words so radically disoriented my identity that I started to live from my true identity as the beloved of God and not out of a false identity created through my own comparisons to the world. David, my name, means "beloved of God." I finally started to believe it. Do you believe this about yourself?

Loving Others

When we allow his song to change our core identity, we become so filled by love that we can honestly and genuinely love others. It's actually how we love God back. When we love God, we love what he loves, and he loves his people and wants us to love them too. In John 21:16, the resurrected Jesus instructs Peter to "take care of my sheep." That's our call too. We love God by taking care of what he loves: his sheep.

How do we do that? He laid down his life for us, so we lay down our lives for him. We yield to his love revealed in Jesus and do what he calls us to do. We love others. We give and we pour out and we challenge and we discipline because we genuinely care. We care because we have been loved and filled. We do so unconditionally. We don't keep score. We love others as a joyful response to the wonder of *being loved*.

Remember, you cannot give what you do not have. To love, you have to be loved. He fills us, and then we fill others. We fill our world with the sweet fragrance and aroma of love, but it's not worldly love—it's life-giving love, transforming love, godly love, because that's who he is. And that's what becomes attractive. That's what will cause Christ's church to grow. When we love others and our community sacrificially, people will be naturally drawn to what they find nowhere else:

Love that gives. Love that sacrifices. Love that is poured out. Love that is countercultural and counterintuitive.

Many years ago it was my pleasure and joy to be loved by a dear friend named Ruff Robinson. Ruff lived on Signal Mountain and belonged to the church I served as a young pastor. I knew nothing about owning a home or fixing anything, so Ruff became my *go-to* friend. One of the first things he taught me was how to dig a posthole so I could put a new mailbox in front of my house. I'll never forget it. No matter the situation, no matter the need, Ruff dropped what he was doing and came to help. Whenever he left, job complete, he thanked me for calling him, for giving him the opportunity to come over and help. Huh? Why was *he* thanking *me*?

Ruff was also an elder in our church, and he often stopped by my office and prayed for me. He inquired about my stress or my struggles, and he gently and lovingly implored the Lord on my behalf. He did this not only for me but for countless others in our community. I was only one of the many whom Ruff loved.

I'm not sure I have ever known anyone who so humbly understood the delight God took in him than Ruff. He loved Jesus and he clearly understood that Jesus loved him. He was an ordinary man with ordinary skills and an ordinary life, but through Christ, he had an extraordinary capacity to love. Because of that, you wanted to be near him. Ruff was *attractive*. He had the same unique understanding that Joel did, and Ruff's understanding of God's love had the same result. He was secure in his identity in Christ, and he was enabled to love. Today there is a mission fund at Signal Mountain Presbyterian Church that celebrates Ruff's life and heart. I'm not nearly as mature as Ruff was, but I hope I can grow as he did. I hope I can grow in understanding God's true delight in me so I can genuinely love and serve others to the glory of God.

A Final Question

In light of the significance of this chapter, I am compelled to ask you a question. It's something Blaise Pascal, a seventeenth-century French mathematician and philosopher, described in his book *Pensées* that became known as "Pascal's Wager." What it says is this: We all need to consider who God is and make a decision based on what has been revealed. The cross of Christ is a fork in the road. Do we believe we are eternally loved by God? As we decide whether we will live as his disciple from this day forward, Pascal's Wager would have us consider:

- If the atheists of our culture are right and I'm wrong, then I've lost nothing. There is no god, no eternity, and no punishment, so I have nothing to fear. This life is all there is. When we die, the atheists and I will have the same fate. We'll be food for worms. While that may be discouraging, there's no long-term negative consequence for me. The atheists and I get the same thing.

- If I'm right and the atheists are wrong, however, then they lose everything. If I'm right and they're wrong, then I live in the light of God's love both now and eternally. However, they won't because they have not received and accepted the sacrificial love that reconciles them to the Father. If there were more than one way to be reconciled, then Jesus would never have died. If other religions could accomplish the same result, then why would God kill his Son for no reason? Intellectually, either Christianity is a joke and I'm nuts for writing this book, or Jesus is the Son of God and my Savior and I'm going to live forever with him.

Are non-Christians willing to make that wager? If they're right and I'm wrong, I'm fine. If I'm right and they're wrong, then they are in a tough spot.

Joel has nothing that the world considers attractive, and yet he is attractive. Joel has every reason to give up on God, yet he doesn't. Joel has every reason to believe he has no value, yet he refuses the lie. His identity is firmly held in God's love, which has so disoriented him away from the world that it redefines every element of how he understands himself. He is a child of the King, beautiful in every way, and he lives that way. He lives out of his true identity. I pray that you will grow in your understanding of God's love so that it will completely disorient you and redefine how you see yourself. In so doing, you'll know love and give love as you never have before.

Who is God? He's love. Let him fill your cup with the wonder and delight he takes in you, and then go and let that love spill from your life into the lives of others.

PART 3

Learning
to Be You
Is a Process

11

Why Is This Taking So Long?

UNDERSTANDING THE PROCESS
OF GROWING IN CHRIST

Now we ask you and urge you in the Lord Jesus to [live to please God] more and more.

1 Thessalonians 4:1

We have become known more as people who preach the gospel than as those who live and adorn it.

John Stott, *Commentary on 1 Thessalonians*

My wife is an amazing woman. Like all smart men, I married way over my head.

Leigh has been a tremendous encouragement to me through the many ups and downs of the past twenty-three years, but she has also been a source of great inspiration. That inspiration has come in a variety of forms, but recently it has come through her faithful service to incarcerated women in our county. I would never have believed it fifteen years ago, but God has a wonderful way of doing the unexpected.

I have gone with her on many occasions, and the only way to describe it is to say she is gifted. God filled her with a passion for serving these women, and then he gave her the natural gifts and ability to do so. It's amazing. I love to watch her in *her world*. She eases through all the security lines and checkpoints, talks to the guards, waves to different inmates in the various pods along the main corridor, and teaches Bible studies in a way that is winsome, inviting, and warm. And the inmates love her.

They also confide in her. The stories told to her on a regular basis are utterly heartbreaking. Many come from abusive homes or abject poverty. Most are addicted to drugs. The drugs create an incessant demand for more money, which often leads to prostitution. The cycle is vicious, and they know it.

Two women's stories stand out. The first woman I'll call Cleo. Cleo was a fairly typical inmate: addicted to drugs and working the streets for customers so she could buy her next hit. Repeated arrests finally led her to an extended jail sentence, so Leigh had the chance to get to know her fairly well. In the weeks they spent together, Cleo came faithfully to weekly Bible studies. She often asked Leigh for private meetings. More questions came in written notes. Over time, she accepted God's love and grace in Christ, and her attitude began to drastically change. She was excited about a new life. Then she was released.

Several weeks later, Leigh arrived to teach her Bible study and there was Cleo, back in jail. Cleo kept her head down, not wanting to look at my wife, but Leigh walked over nonetheless. "Miss Leigh," she said, "I'm so sorry. I'm so sorry. I know I should not be back in here. I wanted to do good. I wanted to follow Jesus, but when I got out, it was different. I don't want to want these things, but the minute I got out, I wanted my drink, my drugs, and my man. Why? Am I not really a Christian? Does God not really love me? Why am I still like this?"

Leigh said, "Cleo, yes, you're a Christian, and yes, God loves you! Don't ever doubt that. You're also human, and learning to live as his disciple takes time. The more you try to love Jesus, the more you'll want what Jesus wants, and you'll change, but you'll still fight the things you used to want. It just takes time."

The Lord knows I have felt like that a thousand times or more. I'm sure you have too. As mentioned in chapter 1, Paul said, "I do not understand what I do. For what I want to do I do not do, but what I hate I do" (Rom. 7:15). I think that sums it up quite well. Welcome to being human. Welcome to the challenge of living out of one's *true* identity.

The second story is a little different. This past Mother's Day, God gave my wife a gift. She left our downtown church with another woman, walking and talking on their way to our parking garage. As they walked the two blocks, she noticed a young woman walking ahead of them, tattoos up and down both arms, worn-out clothes, and a walk that suggested deep fatigue. As they continued their conversation, the woman ahead suddenly turned around and shouted, "Miss Leigh, Miss Leigh, it's Cherry. I'm Cherry from the jail. I was in your Bible class. I was walking along and I heard your voice and I thought that just had to be you! Do you remember me?"

Startled, my wife said, "Cherry, I'm glad to see you! Tell me what you're doing." Cherry explained, "Well, those Bible classes really changed me. I realized I needed to get my life together, so I got out and started trying to live more like Jesus. It's taken a long time, but I've changed a lot. I've been out for more than a year, and I'm trying. I rode the bus downtown so I could perform my community service hours as part of my sentence. I have to clean the parking garage today. But it's okay. I'm good. My life is so much better, and I can't thank you enough for helping me get on the right track."

What a gift. Cherry had taken the Word of God to heart, and while her life was not perfect, she was seeing the transformation of the Holy Spirit at work within her. She isn't who she was, and she's not who she is going to be either, but she is on the way. I'm not sure I've seen my wife smile as big as she did when she got home that day.

Those two stories highlight the challenges of *learning to be you*. It's hard. It takes time. Sometimes we get frustrated, but if we keep trusting God, we *will* see change. Transformation *does* happen, but we can't expect it to happen all at once. Accepting Christ and living for him does not wave a magic wand over your human heart that takes away all your struggles with sinful desire. It's a process of slow, steady growth that when followed over time yields great transformation and a life that bears fruit for the kingdom of God. That's what we're aiming for.

Motivated by Love

If that slow, steady change is going to occur in us, we have to recognize the basis and power for that change. Our desire to live for Christ grows as a result of our love for him. Our lives become the expression of our love. When we grasp how God loves us, we desire to love him back. We want to respond to what he has given.

Let me make a small confession: I have an unhealthy love for French fries. My particular favorites are the chili-cheese fries at Snuffer's Restaurant in Dallas, but taste in fries varies. Some prefer a thin, crispy fry like they make at Steak 'n Shake, while others prefer a meatier, softer fry such as what you find at Wendy's or Burger King. On the national landscape, McDonald's is the champion of the French fry. In numerous surveys over the past ten years, Americans have said they prefer McDonald's fries hands-down, and there's a reason for that: McDonald's has some of the most exacting French fry standards in the world.

Not just any potato can become a McDonald's French fry. They buy 3 billion pounds of potatoes each year, scouring the world and testing which brand of potatoes will stand up to the legacy of being a McDonald's fry. Naturally, because of their powerful position in the industry, they largely determine whether a certain variety of potato winds up in your bag at the drive-thru window or goes to the far less lucrative crinkle-cut potato section in your grocer's freezer or, even worse, becomes the dreaded potato chip—the lowest rung on the potato food chain. According to Jeanne Debons, director of the Potato Variety Management Institute, "It's a card game where McDonald's holds nine-tenths of the cards."[1] See, you didn't even know there was such an institute, did you?

Knowing this, what do you think motivates potato farmers? They want to please McDonald's. If a farmer can please McDonald's, it means a huge financial windfall. So naturally, farmers *love* McDonald's. They work every year to come up with new varieties of potatoes in the hope of winning McDonald's favor. The Premier Russet potato, an ancestor of the buff-skinned Penobscot potato of Maine, was developed for just this reason. The Canadian Shepody and the Russet Burbanks also came about because of this.[2] Why? Potato farmers love McDonald's, and so they work hard to demonstrate that love. Their love for McDonald's brings about change.

When you and I love someone, we naturally want to please him or her. Just like those farmers, we want to do things that are going to make our beloved happy. Last year I threw a surprise birthday party for my wife. I did that because I love her and wanted to do something that would please her. Now to be sure, our desire to please others may not always be motivated by love, but many times it is.

In light of this truth, let me ask you a few questions:

Who are you trying to please these days?

Who or what do you love to the extent that your behavior is altered in some way?

Are you trying to please your boss because you see that as a means to a better financial end?

Are you trying to please others in your social group so they will like you and accept you and include you?

Are you trying to please yourself, doing what you want because pleasing yourself is the most important thing?

Or, from a heart motivated by love, do you think about how you can please your spouse, your children, and your friends?

Most of all, does it ever occur to you, in the course of any given day, to try to live in a way that pleases God because you love him?

To be honest, pleasing God is not my first thought. Most mornings I don't get out of bed and think, *God, I love you so much that today I want to please you.* Far more often I get out of bed and think, *David, you've had a rough week, how can I make you feel better?* Maybe I have messed up at home and need to get out of the doghouse, so I think, *What can I do to please Leigh?* Even then, such thoughts are motivated by *my* needs more than hers.

When it comes to our relationship with God, we have managed to compartmentalize it in such a way that our love for God is expressed primarily on Sunday, or perhaps in a crisis, but rarely on a daily basis. We are grateful to know we are loved and forgiven, but we have let go of the notion that our love for God should have any significant impact on our behavior. This, of course, is illustrated by the data that tells us that Christian behavior and secular behavior are no different. We divorce at the same rate. We give to charities and nonprofits at the same rate. We are involved in pornography at the same rate. And the list goes on. Our walk does not appear to match our talk. God loves us, but we seem to be missing the corresponding change that happens when we love him back.

Learning to Love God Back

Paul speaks to this in 1 Thessalonians 4:1–11. Paul, Timothy, and Silas founded the church in that city, but because of strong opposition, they had to flee for their lives in the middle of the project. They never had the chance to say proper good-byes, so this first letter is an explanation from Paul to his followers about his behavior, about the nature of the gospel, and about the accusations being levied against him in that city. As Paul begins chapter 4, he talks about the manifestation of their faith in their public behavior.

He effectively raises some of the questions I have posed here. Who were the Thessalonian Christians trying to please? It is a challenging question for us to examine as we think about what it truly means to *walk* with Jesus Christ as his disciple, grappling with the frustrations that go along with such pursuit.

At the outset, Paul makes it clear that when we truly love God, we should also try to please him, and what pleases him is when we do what he asks. Paul writes in the first verse, "Brothers and sisters, we instructed you how to live in order to please God. . . . Now we ask you and urge you in the Lord Jesus to do this more and more" (1 Thess. 4:1). Ouch. Paul says we are to love God, and if we do, there should be a corresponding adjustment in our behavior. The instructions have been given clearly, and God's desire for us is to heed those instructions. This is the root of Christian ethics. It is why we act differently than the rest of the world.

The problem is that our world does not function that way. We live in a world in which absolute truth is denied. There is no single way to live, no absolute set of instructions, therefore everyone makes choices based on what he or she believes to be true. Truth is relative. The very notion of obedience is foreign because we are led to believe the highest authority is self. We are the ones who govern and dictate our affairs, and we get used to that message. Then we come to the gospel and find God calling for obedience to his instructions as an expression of our love, and it feels foreign. We're not used to yielding to any other truth other than our own perception of it.

Out of that understanding, we enter Christian faith. We want to talk about the parts of the gospel that reveal God's love for us and God's forgiveness of us. We want to talk about God's presence and God's peace in our lives. That's the gospel we want to preach. In our modern-day culture of abundant personal pleasures and freedoms, like everyone else, we want to be free to please ourselves. We want to be forgiven, but we don't want to be bothered with how we're living and the choices we're making. John Stott writes in his commentary:

> We have become known more as people who preach the gospel than as those who live and adorn it. At least in the statistics on marriage and family life, Jewish performance is higher than that of Christians. One of the main reasons for this is

192

our churches do not teach ethics. We are so busy preaching the gospel that we seldom teach the law.[3]

In our Christian lives, there's a twofold call: we need to trust Christ and receive his forgiveness, but we also need to live as if that means something to us because God has made known to us what pleases him. He is pleased when we obey him.

For example, there are certain things I ask my children to do. They know when they do what I say, it will make me happy. The issue is how they deal with their stuff. Call us crazy, but Leigh and I expect them to pick up what belongs to them and take it upstairs. We ask them all the time, but it never seems to happen. They wonder why we get upset. Here's why: If they tell us they love us and they know what we want them to do, yet they never do it, what sort of message does that send? It says, "Mom and Dad, you're really not that important. We love you—but not enough to do what you ask."

Do you see how this applies to our lives in Christ? God makes it plain how he expects us to behave. Paul instructs the Thessalonians at length about how they are supposed to live, but they aren't doing it, so he calls them on it. Your obedience is an expression of your love for God, and your obedience pleases him.

Before you assume I am trying to turn your faith into a legalistic, rule-following religion, that's not it at all. I am not talking about living your life with an obsession for following rules because you fear what may happen if you don't. It's not about following rules; it's about loving the Ruler back by trying to please him. There's a huge difference. When we truly love God, it is going to be the most natural thing in the world to want to please him. We don't live our lives wringing our hands, obsessed by all the rules we must follow and things we must do. Instead, we think about the love poured out for us in Christ and about living in a way that honors him. As we do that more and more, what pleases him pleases us. It is the process of our spiritual growth and maturity. It's slow and it's steady, but it's utterly wonderful as you see it unfold in your life.

Far From Perfect

Naturally, we are not perfect in this. In our sinful nature, we are motivated not to please God but to please ourselves. So we should always understand our obedience as a work in progress. Paul says, "Do this more and more. . . . It is God's will that you should be sanctified" (1 Thess. 4:1, 3). God wants us to be sanctified, but what does that mean?

Paul has already established in previous letters that the presence of the Holy Spirit in our lives is for the purpose of our Christlikeness. God wants to shape us into the image of his Son, Jesus. "For those God foreknew he also predestined to be conformed to the image [likeness] of his Son" (Rom. 8:29). From the foundations of the world, God has chosen us in Christ so that we can be *conformed to his likeness*. God wants us to be like Jesus. When we trust God by faith, *his* expectation and plan is that such transformation will happen.

The hard reality, however, is that such transformation does not happen overnight. As indicated in 1 Thessalonians 4:1, we become that way "more and more." It happens gradually. We are more like Christ than we were yesterday, but we are not as much like Christ as we will be tomorrow. We are a work in progress.

One year I attended a conference where they handed out buttons to each attendee that said "PBPGINFWMY." The letters stood for: Please Be Patient, God Is Not Finished With Me Yet. What a wonderful expression of our true human condition. By the Holy Spirit, we are all works in progress. We get it and then we lose it. We act with love and compassion, and then we act selfishly. It's never all one or the other. While my frustration with the lack of permanent change goes on, I am encouraged by the explanation. At least I know what I am experiencing is quite normal in the Christian journey.

The even better news comes from Paul's words in Philippians 1:6, "Being confident of this, that he who began a good work in you will carry it on to completion until the day of Christ Jesus." We are incomplete works, yes, but God is going to finish the work. He is going to complete us when we meet him in glory, and that is a promise that emboldens and encourages us in this process.

Part of our growth, then, is to understand the process. We are being "sanctified" (1 Thess. 4:3). Sometimes we get to that word and trip up a bit because it sounds so big and fancy. In anyone's spiritual journey in Christ, there are three things that happen: justification, sanctification, and glorification. Your *justification* happens at the moment you receive Christ as your Savior and become redeemed by his blood. His righteousness is imputed to you, and therefore you stand as one justified before God. Paul writes, "For all have sinned and fall short of the glory of God, and all are justified freely by his grace through the redemption that came by Christ Jesus" (Rom. 3:23–24). Your sins are no longer held against you; they have been placed on Christ.

Glorification is what happens at the end. When you die or when Jesus comes back, glorification is your reward. That's when you drop your physical body as well as an existence in human time and space and you go to live in glory. You receive your glorified body in Christ, you become recognizable to all who dwell in heaven, and that glory never ends. (I love it when Peter sees Moses and Elijah on the Mount of

Transfiguration in Luke 9:28–36. He's never met either one of them, and Jesus never says who they are. Yet in their glory, Peter knows them.)

In between your justification and your glorification is your *sanctification*. It is the process by which God, having redeemed you in Christ, transforms your life and heart so that you increasingly want what God wants. Your heart starts to reflect *his* heart, and that process happens for the rest of your life. Think about it. Are you more like Christ than you were five years ago? Two years ago? Are you more like Christ today than you were six weeks ago, and if not, why?

For this exact reason, every three years I ask our elders to write out their testimony. I ask them to reflect on God's work in their lives over the past three years. Initially some say, "I did that three years ago. Why do I have to do it again?" My answer is: because the story of God's work in our lives is a gradually unfolding one that changes over time. Your testimony is more than "I grew up in a Christian home." It's the story of what God did in transforming you in the past year; it's the story of how you are more like Christ today than you were three years ago. If we never take the time to think about this, we miss the actual growth. Take that time!

Clearly we're not perfect, but as our heart seeks to love God back, we try to do what pleases him. As the Holy Spirit empowers us, we "more and more" do what he says as a joyful response to our salvation. Yes, we'll trip and fall, but we get back up, confess our sins, and resolve again to be *his* disciple. God knows us. He does not expect us to ever arrive at perfection. He knows we're not perfect, yet he does expect us to move in *his* direction—to do it more and more. As each day passes, one building on the next, we grow. We change. We transform more and more into the person God wants us to be—a living, breathing witness to the love and grace of Jesus.

As a parent, I have loved watching the growth of my children through the years. It is a true joy to see them develop as people, to see the human beings God is shaping them to be. At various points, however, I didn't fault them for being where they were on that journey. We don't blame babies for crying. That's what babies do. When my son was four, I did not get angry with him that his vocabulary was so limited. When my daughter was eleven, I did not grow frustrated with her that she giggled and squealed a lot. (That's what junior high girls do, right?) I understood that my children were moving through a process of maturing, and my expectations reflected that. But if my son had been unable to speak in complete sentences at sixteen, then I would have recognized a problem. I didn't expect growth all at once, but I did expect progress.

So it is in our relationship with God. He does not expect us to be spiritual giants immediately, but he does expect and desire our growth—our maturity—as we grasp what it means to be a disciple of Jesus.

A Hard Example

Given the culture we live in, I need to point out the example that Paul uses for illustrating his teaching. He uses our sexual expression to make his point. He says our sexual behavior should be a reflection of our faithful and eternal love for God. Out of all the examples Paul could have picked to illustrate this point about sanctification, why pick this one? Why go there?

Here's why: Thessalonica was famous for sexual immorality. The Greco-Roman world at that time was filled with pagan sexual rituals, not to mention the well-accepted notion that men did not have to limit themselves to their wife as their only sexual partner. F. F. Bruce writes, "A man might have a mistress, a concubine, and a harlot with each one fulfilling different duties. His wife was to manage the household and be the mother to his legitimate children and heirs."[4] Into that culture—one that sounds painfully like our own—God says, "Each of you should learn to control your own body in a way that is holy and honorable, not in passionate lust" (1 Thess. 4:4–5). We are called to love God, and we love him by doing what pleases him, and what pleases him is when we do what he says. And God is pleased when we control our bodies so that they honor him.

This is not the practice of our culture today. Far from anything that resembles *more and more* control, it is *less and less* control. We are allowing our physical bodies to be used as billboards for passionate lust, and it may well be the greatest single expression that reveals how much we love ourselves and how little we love the Lord. My own paraphrase of what Paul says is this: "Live a life that is pleasing to God. In fact, the greatest example of how you can do that is to stop living like the culture, with no control in regard to sex, and start controlling yourselves so you honor God." I pray that we will learn from this and reflect seriously on what pleases God so we can begin to live according to a Christian ethic and not one of our own making.

Gratefully, Paul moves from the negative example to the positive one. Instead of losing control of our bodies, what are we supposed to do? Love each other. Paul writes, "You yourselves have been taught by God to love each other. . . . We urge you . . . to do so more and more" (1 Thess. 4:9–10). There it is again. More and more, in an ever-increasing fashion, we are to love.

What was the model of Christ? Love. Not spineless, cheap love but gracious, sacrificial love. God is pleased when we do what he says, and what he says is, "Love each other," which is defined by our behavior. Dallas Willard writes in his book *Knowing Christ Today*, "You cannot succeed in being ethical in act or character unless you have abandoned having your way, fulfilling your own desires, as the rule of your life. That is the ethical meaning of love as taught and practiced by Jesus."[5]

True love for God—acting in a truly loving way—is shown when we stop trying to please ourselves and start trying to please him. That's what Jesus did, isn't it? Facing the cross, he said, "Not my will, but yours be done" (Luke 22:42). Jesus loved us well because he yielded *his* will to the will of the Father.

Where It Gets Real

This is the *rubber meets the road* part of Christian faith. It's not easy because we don't naturally want to do what God wants, especially in a culture where that is so different from the norm. People are going to look at us like we're nuts. They are going to reject us and persecute us and laugh at the standards we keep. Our choice of music or dance or generosity or movies or friends may not be the norm. But here's the thing: it all comes from loving God. In his sermon called "Prodigal Love for the Prodigal Son," Charles Spurgeon says:

> Some of us know what it is like to be too happy to live. The love of God has been so overpoweringly experienced by us on some occasions that we almost have to ask God to stop the delight because we could endure no more. If God had not shielded His love and glory a bit, we believe we could not have stood it.[6]

What a moment for Spurgeon, to know of God's love in such a defining way. Does that sound like a man who got all hung up on following rules? Of course not. When we are loved by God, it is so rich and fulfilling that nothing else matters. We want to please him, and if we displease someone else in the process or find ourselves being cast off or rejected as a result, then so be it. Nothing is more amazing than when we experience the overpowering love of God in our lives.

Don't get hung up on not being where Spurgeon was spiritually when he spoke those words. He was years into *his* walk with Christ. I remember having a painful conversation with a young man in our church who had accepted Christ after some very rough living. He was addicted to several things, but he recognized his deep need for Christ and committed his life to Jesus on the spot. He got into Alcoholics Anonymous, started attending church and Bible study regularly, built relationships with other Christians, and was generally doing everything he could to follow Christ.

When he came to my office, he was in tears. "Why," he asked me, "does the Lord not take away these desires? Why do I still keep doing these things? Am I a Christian?" I'm not sure I've ever seen a man whose heart so purely and deeply wanted to follow Christ and who was so utterly pained by his failure to do so. I found myself saying the same things that my wife said to Cleo a few weeks earlier: "Joe, you're new at this. You have only been walking with Christ for a number of weeks. Yes, God can do miracles, but those are uncommon moments. The reality is that walking with Christ is a daily yielding of your will to the will of the Father as you seek to love him. The more you do that, the more you will want what he wants. The more you do that, the less you will desire the things of this world. Don't try to make it all happen today. Don't get frustrated that you are not the man you are going to be a year from now. It takes time. Let the Holy Spirit have *his* way in you, and trust that God is at work."

Contrary to what we hear at times, receiving Christ does not always mean the story has a perfect ending. Christ inhabits sinful people. The war is over, but we still fight the daily battles with the enemy. Joe kept going, and each day as he sought God's direction in his life, God was faithful in meeting his needs and providing the necessary support to beat his addictions. Does that mean all his desire for those things is gone? Of course not. It does mean that he is being sanctified, that he is trying to live for real every day as a follower of Jesus Christ.

I have a friend who uses an expression almost every week as we talk and share about our lives: "Just keep loading the wagon." In other words, there's a lot of work that needs to be done in us—the wagon is big and there's a lot that needs to be loaded. If we just keep loading it, however, before too long we'll look up and realize we've actually made a lot of progress. God is at work. God is faithful. God will one day complete each and every one of us, but we're not there yet.

Don't get frustrated. Focus on the abundant, lavish manner in which God has loved you in Jesus Christ, and then joyfully respond to that love. Love him back. More and more, yield your will to his will. Every day, keep loading the wagon of faithful obedience, and you'll find, as the years pass, that you look more and more like Jesus.

12

Unashamed

WHY LIVING FOR CHRIST
IS COUNTER TO OUR CULTURE

I am not ashamed of the gospel, because it is the power of
God that brings salvation to everyone who believes.

Romans 1:16

A poor, poor imitation I am, or wish to be, but in this service
I hope to live. In it, I wish to die.

David Livingstone, medical missionary

He is no fool who gives what he cannot keep to gain what
he cannot lose.

Jim Elliot, missionary and Christian martyr

We can all benefit from a healthy dose of perspective at times—those cage-rattling moments that
reorient our minds away from what presently consumes us

and refocuses us on the larger issues being experienced by many in our world. I had one of those moments last weekend.

A missionary couple visited our church. They were home on furlough, traveling through the United States to raise prayer and financial support. What made them unique was the location of their missionary service: Kabul, Afghanistan. They were serving the Lord in arguably one of the most dangerous and impoverished parts of the world.

For security reasons, I'll call them Ruth and Peter. Ruth and Peter had been typical citizens of the world, creating a successful business that brought them a comfortable life for many years. Then they met Jesus and everything changed. Disoriented by his sacrificial love, they committed their lives to serving him. Even when the call came to serve in Afghanistan, they answered without hesitation.

Listening to them describe the daily routine of their lives was inspiring beyond measure. Then they told the even more amazing story of an Islamic man we'll call Sameh, who is married with four children, and who accepted Jesus and became a Christian. Like many newly converted believers, he was zealous in his love for the Lord and his desire to serve him. Even in a country where such conversions are distinctly frowned upon, Sameh made it known that he followed Jesus.

Word spread. He was rejected by many and vilified in his community. Authorities threatened him with punishment if he persisted, yet he refused to stop. Joyfully, he shared with others. The authorities put him in jail. Still he continued witnessing. He shared the gospel with the guards and the other prisoners, including a member of the Taliban in the next cell. For this offense, he was beaten almost daily. He was tortured in ways too terrible to describe in these pages. All this was done in an effort to break his affirmation of faith in Jesus Christ.

Every day Ruth and Peter visited him, witnessing the hor-rific results of the beatings. Every day Ruth, Peter, and Sameh prayed together. While the beatings continued, he refused to recant. One night the Taliban inmate had a dream. He saw a vision of Jesus dressed in white, radiant in his glory. In the dream, Jesus told the man he needed to listen to Sameh. Sameh awoke that night to the sight of the Taliban man kneeling at the edge of his cell saying, "I have seen Jesus, and he told me to talk to you."

That night Sameh led the man to the Lord. Miraculously, God intervened and Sameh was released from prison after nine months. His family was rescued, flown out of the coun-try, and reunited with Sameh in another location after several weeks. Today they are safe and secure, continuing to serve and honor the Lord with their lives.

Ruth and Peter described Sameh's attitude through the entire experience as one of constant humility, joy, and grati-tude. In spite of his great physical pain, the presence of the Lord was sufficient for him to endure the abuse. It was unlike anything Peter or Ruth had ever witnessed. When I shared this with our congregation, I was overcome by emotion and started to weep. Then when I introduced Peter and Ruth to our church, they all rose to their feet applauding. It was a holy, sacred moment—a perspective moment that reoriented all of us to what our Christian journey is all about.

In the days that followed, I could not get a troublesome question out of my mind. Perhaps the same question has already occurred to you. If I had been in Sameh's position, what would I have done? Would I have been willing to endure such terrible circumstances in order to remain faithful to my confession of faith in Jesus Christ? Most of us will never know the answer to that question because we will not find ourselves in that position. Yet the reality is that we face the same challenge nearly every day, although the consequences are less severe. Most of us are not being physically threatened or facing imprisonment if we don't stop talking about Jesus, but we do face cultural opposition in a variety of troubling ways.

In today's culture, living in an authentic manner that honors Christ means we will face accusations of being exclusive and narrow. We will be made to feel ignorant by those who consider themselves intellectually elite, those who believe that faith in God is scientifically untenable. We will be accused of being judgmental if we do not approve of or condone certain behaviors or actions or beliefs. If we speak openly, we will be labeled as "one of those Jesus freaks" or be accused of violating someone's personal rights. These consequences can come at us from anywhere: family members, co-workers, friends, neighbors. Because we often know the sources well, we feel belittled, rejected, and insecure. Doubts are raised in our minds. *Maybe they're right*, we think. *Maybe I'm not seeing this right.*

With the seed of doubt now firmly planted, we compromise. We yield. We find ourselves on the sidelines of faith, not actually in the game. We'd rather blend in and be liked, so that's what we do. We don't talk about Jesus much. Consequently, we forget that following Christ is a daily commitment. We live in the same way the culture does. When we come home, we feel torn. The internal conflict is real. We believe in Jesus. We love God, but we seem to lack the power to live the way Sameh did, authentically sharing the gospel of Jesus Christ. Rather than yielding to the will and call of God, we yield to the opinions and pressures of those around us.

I'm a pastor, and I feel that way at times. I feel enormously guilty when an opportunity to openly live for Christ comes and I don't take it. I imagine you do as well. I said in the last chapter that living for real takes time, but it also takes courage—courage born of our perspective on the larger kingdom of God. If we are going to become more like Christ, then we need to examine the roots of our reluctance to live faithfully. What is it we're afraid of? What creates the reluctance to live authentically and openly for Jesus?

The Power of Shame

Several months ago I did something I rarely ever do: I went to the mall to shop with my wife. This is an endeavor that I find particularly exhausting, but I thought it might score me enough points for a later round of golf, so I went. After thirty minutes I was totally depleted and asked if we could stop for lunch, which we did. I had a delicious vegetable plate (that's doubtful—I probably had French fries) and then asked for our check. I'm not sure exactly what happened at that point, but it felt like they forgot us. The check didn't show up.

Ever the creative one, I saw this as a possible way to avoid more shopping, so I said, "Honey, why don't you go on to the next store, and I'll wait here until the check comes." She said that was fine, but then she threw me a curve ball. She said, "There are some things I want to look at in that store, and I don't want to have to watch my purse. Will you bring it with you?" What was I supposed to say? It was an innocent request, but not one I was thrilled about doing. Since I felt the guilt of my original plan to avoid shopping, I reluctantly agreed, and off she went.

The store where she had gone was not far away, but my fragile male ego did not want any part of walking around that restaurant and then the mall with a purse over my arm. I tried to think of a way to attach a sign to it that said, "This is my wife's purse," or, "Quit staring. This is a European man bag." Out of options, I took her purse and headed for the door. As I did, I thought to myself, *You know, this is a little embarrassing, but so be it. Leigh is more important to me than what other people may think.*

No doubt I was trying to talk myself into that, but it was true. I felt kind of odd as I walked along, but I was willing to feel that way because I love my wife. A little discomfort or shame didn't seem too much to ask. It was also not the first time in my relationship with Leigh that my love for her trumped any feelings of potential shame or embarrassment. Consider that while we were dating, I played the guitar and sang "The Wedding Song" to her while seated on a blanket in a public park with people walking all around us. Talk about shameful. I didn't care. I was in love with this woman, and that was all that mattered!

Here's what I've learned: *Love trumps shame.* Always has, always will. Sometimes we do crazy things or things we would not normally do, risking personal shame because of our love for another. Shame can be a powerful emotion. Most of us know at least a little bit of what that feels like. Loosely defined, shame is "a painful emotion resulting from an awareness of inadequacy or guilt in front of others; a state of dishonor."[1]

External forces are brought to bear on our lives so that we feel inadequate or guilty, and those feelings are compounded by the fact that others know the situation. We feel as though we have been dishonored in the eyes of the world. When my grandfather died in New York many years ago, I felt tremendous shame when I elected not to attend his funeral. Given the panic attacks I had been experiencing, I could not bear the thought of getting on an airplane, so everyone in my family went but me, and I felt ashamed. Even knowing what I know today about God's love and grace, I can *still* feel that shame. It is powerful.

We know that honest, gut-level feeling of shame, and it has significant application to our faith and how we live as disciples of Jesus Christ. As our culture moves further and further away from a Christian foundation, those who possess faith are often made to feel ashamed of what we believe. That is the root of our reluctance. It's why we find ourselves falling back or closing up or blending in. It's a powerful feeling, and we want to avoid it. So as we think about living as disciples of Jesus Christ, how do we learn to cope with this? How do we live authentically as disciples of Jesus in a world that can often induce feelings of shame in us?

Love Trumps Shame

Strong answers are found to these questions in the beginning of Paul's most complete theological work: his letter to the Romans. Rome was a city Paul had long desired to visit, but for a variety of reasons he had been unable to do so. Given that Rome was the center of the world and recognizing its strategic importance to the spread of the gospel, Paul wrote this letter to provide a solid theological foundation on which the church in Rome could stand—a foundation greatly needed because Roman culture was mostly opposed to and offended by the gospel.

This concept was common in Paul's writings. In 1 Corinthians 1:23, Paul wrote that the gospel was "a stumbling block to Jews and foolishness to Gentiles." The Gentiles heard the gospel as being nothing but foolishness. It was an outlandish, even shameful idea to suggest that a mighty God not only became a human being but also was humiliated to such an extent that he allowed himself to be executed in the most shameful manner: crucifixion. In Gentile circles, such an idea was viewed as almost obscene. So anyone like Paul who proclaimed that message was viewed with great disdain. The idea of the gospel was shameful to most Gentiles, which meant it was a tough audience for Paul to reach—an audience quite similar to the culture in which we live today.

Our culture is trying hard to minimize the significance of the cross. It is viewed as one truth among many possible options. Believing the gospel as a singular, authoritative truth for all time may mean we who actually try to follow and obey Christ are looked upon as being fools. So if that's the case, how do we cope?

We cope by first recognizing that such feelings can be overcome. It's a given that others will attack us and attempt to shame us, but we don't have to accept the shame they seek to impart. We overcome the shame by the depth and purity of our love for God. *Remember, love trumps shame.* Paul writes in Romans 1:9, "The God whom I serve with all my heart by preaching the Good News about his Son" (GNT). Paul served God with his whole heart. He held nothing back. He loved God completely, and I think the reason he did was that he recognized the depth of God's love for him.

Paul met the Lord on the road to Damascus (Acts 9). He saw God's power firsthand. In spite of the fact that Paul had lived for years as one actively opposed to the gospel, God, in his infinite grace, redeemed Paul's life and transformed his heart. Because of that, Paul was all in. There was nothing Paul would not do for God because he was acutely and deeply aware of what he had been redeemed from. He knew the extent of God's love.

When we live in the purity of relationship with God, daily drenched in his love, any potential feeling of shame that may come over us pales in comparison. We get a glimpse of this in Genesis 2:25: "Adam and his wife were both naked, and they felt no shame." Have you ever wondered why that was the case? They felt no shame because they were clothed in the purity and the glory of God's abiding love. Sin had not entered yet. There was nothing but love in the purity of that moment, and so there was no shame.

It's not an easy feeling to overcome, but through Christ we can overcome shame. I have great respect for a certain man in my church. Like many, he lost his job two years ago in the worst part of the recession. Money was tight. He had a wife and two children to support. Things got so bad that when their second car broke down, they could not afford to fix it. Needing work, but with his wife needing their remaining car to get to her job as well as their need to take care of their children, he took a job cleaning buildings from midnight to 8 a.m. Every day, he rode a bike as his means of transportation, sweating through twelve miles each way.

Everything in our culture says, "You did what? You have a job doing what?" I know he struggled with his own pride in it, but he was at church every Sunday. Why did he do it? Love trumps shame. Not only did his love for his wife and kids trump any fear he had of what the world might think, but his love for God trumped shame and pride as well. He did what he had to do. Thankfully for that family, those days have passed. If we want to live faithfully as disciples of Jesus Christ, we must deepen our relationship with him so that our love for him will always supersede any fear we have of what others may think or do. Sameh knew that love, and I think we can know it too.

Keeping Our Eye on the Ball

One of the challenges with this goes back to the issue of perspective. Because we often see the world through the wrong lens, our perspective is warped. We don't see clearly or we look at the wrong things altogether. I'll never forget going through an extended shooting slump as a high school basketball player. At the time, basketball was my life. I was a starter on a good team with a chance to make the playoffs, but suddenly I couldn't throw the ball into the ocean. The longer it went, the more psychological it became. I think my coach was as frustrated as I was. One day in practice, following a series of missed shots, he asked me, "David, when you go to shoot the ball, what are you looking at?" I had to think about it. I said, "Coach, I'm not totally sure." I looked generally at the basket, but I had no clear focus. He said, "Pick out a spot on the front of the rim and try to drop the ball right over it."

As simple as that sounds, it worked. When I went from seeing a lot of things all at once to seeing one exact point, it made all the difference. Slump over. (No, we did not make the playoffs.) This is an essential element in living authentically for Christ. What or who are we looking at? Do we have a clear focus and understanding of the purpose of our lives? We learn to live out of our true identity, as those unashamed of the gospel, when our perspective focuses clearly on the bigger picture of the kingdom of God.

Paul writes, "I am not ashamed of the gospel, because it is the power of God that brings salvation to everyone who believes" (Rom. 1:16). Paul communicates that regardless of the stakes or the cost, he is not going to focus on the opinions of others. His focus is going to be on the kingdom of God because it is a life-and-death matter. The gospel is the only hope of salvation. Therefore everything else, every other opinion, pales in comparison. Nothing else matters.

If you don't see it that way, then you won't live that way. If you put yourself in a theological camp that believes Jesus is just one way of many ways to God, then you will risk nothing for it. It's not worth it. But if you believe that someone else may eternally live or die based on whether they hear what you know to be true in the Bible, then the potential risk of sharing the gospel is *overwhelmed* by its importance. You'll risk shame.

This is highlighted in Romans 1:14 when Paul says, "I am obligated both to Greeks and non-Greeks, both to the wise and the foolish." That may sound like a throwaway line, but it reveals with great clarity what was happening in the culture. The Greek word translated as "non-Greeks" is actually the word *barbaroi*—or "barbarian." It is a word that carries a very derogatory meaning. A barbarian refers to a speaker of a strange or unintelligible language, one who was unsophisticated or beneath another, one who possessed little value or worth.

When Paul says, "I am obligated to barbarians as much as I am to you," he is essentially saying, "Look, there is a larger picture to keep in mind here. The gospel is for everyone, and if you are going to think less of me because I share it with those you think are beneath you, then you are completely missing what the gospel is all about." It's why I got involved in HIV and AIDS ministry back in the late 1980s when people still didn't know what it was or how you could catch it. I believed it was a life-and-death crisis for those patients. A large percentage of them were rejected by their friends and families, largely out of the shame associated with the illness. They were alone, and I believed that was where God wanted the gospel to be shared.

We don't like to admit it, but we can feel that others are beneath us, either by behavior or social position. We subconsciously want to avoid being seen with certain people for fear of what others may think. Paul says we should never look over or around those who do not speak our language, those who are culturally viewed as being in a low position, or those rejected by the culture altogether. Living for Christ means we are not ashamed of the gospel, but it also means we are not ashamed to share it with all those God has made. We go to those who have been shamed by the world and share the gospel. Why? We go because we are unashamed, consumed by our understanding of the larger kingdom of God and by the knowledge that there are lives to be won or lost in the spiritual battle of this world.

Equipped by Prayer

If we want to do anything in this life that is truly of God, then we must never rely on our own strength or will to accomplish it. We must yield to God's strength and power alive within us through his Holy Spirit. To live as those unashamed of the gospel, prayer must be at the center of our relationship with Christ. Paul writes, "I remember you in my prayers at all times; and I pray that . . . the way may be opened for me to come to you" (Rom. 1:9–10). He also says in verse 9, "God . . . is my witness."

Making such a statement reveals Paul's confidence in the Lord. Think about that. How often do you hear someone say, "As God is my witness . . ."? When you say that, either you don't have a clue as to the significance of those words or you have complete confidence in what you are saying because you have been in the presence of God. In spite of the fact that many in that culture thought Paul was a fool, he was able to overcome any shame that he might have felt because he had so faithfully been in the presence of God.

It is true that you will most often bend toward those with whom you spend the most time. Mark 1:35 says, "Very early in the morning, while it was still dark, Jesus got up, left the house and went off to a solitary place, where he prayed." The model of Jesus's ministry was one centered in prayer no matter how busy or how much he was in demand. He was with God, so Jesus always bent in God's direction. He always leaned into doing God's will and nothing else. In spite of that clear model, how do we spend our time? In a single day, an average American will commute 45 minutes, be interrupted 73 times, receive 600 advertising messages, and watch 4 hours of television.[2] We're on the computer, on our phone, at the beach, with our friends, at our job—you name it.

Naturally, you are going to be concerned about what the people you spend time with think. You are going to bend in their direction. Your priority will be to know no shame before them. When you are with God through faithful prayer, however, your priorities change. You become more concerned about what he thinks and what he says and what matters to him *because you've been with him.*

This raises an obvious question: Of all those we spend time with or want to please, which one matters the most? Are you so concerned about what others think of you that you feel ashamed and shrink from the gospel? Or are you so loved by God and in love with God that your heart burns to serve him? It's a question we need to answer because the answer has consequences for our lives.

God is serious about this. Jesus says, "If anyone is ashamed of me and my words in this adulterous and sinful generation, the Son of Man will be ashamed of them when he comes in his Father's glory with the holy angels" (Mark 8:38). God tells us that if we cannot stand securely and courageously for him, then he won't stand for us. God's Word can be hard at times, and following Christ is not always easy. The blessings and rewards of following him far outweigh any consequences, but we have to spend time with God to maintain our perspective on that truth. And we spend time with him primarily through prayer.

God has called us to be his faithful disciples, and when we gain a larger perspective on what truly matters in life, we won't care much about earthly shame. What matters is whether our heavenly Father will say to us on that day, "Well done, good and faithful servant!" (Matt. 25:21).

Hebrews 12:2 reminds us that we should be "fixing our eyes on Jesus, the [author] and perfecter of faith. For the joy set before him he endured the cross, scorning its shame." Jesus endured the shame because of the larger picture of the joy set before him, and when he lives in us, that's how we are called to live. Because of the joy set before us, we live unashamed of the gospel. He has taken our shame—our sin—our darkness. As a result, living for his honor and glory becomes the focus of our lives and the source of our joy.

Many years ago, I came across some words purportedly written by an African pastor who was about to be killed for his refusal to denounce his faith in Christ. To my knowledge, no one has been able to substantiate authorship, but that does not minimize the power of the words:

> I am part of the Fellowship of the Unashamed. I have Holy Spirit power. The die has been cast. I've stepped over the line. The decision has been made. I am a disciple of His. I won't look back, let up, slow down, back away, or be still. My past is redeemed, my present makes sense, and my future is secure.
>
> I am finished and done with low living, sight walking, small planning, smooth knees, colorless dreams, tame visions, mundane talking, chintzy giving, and dwarfed goals! I no longer need preeminence, prosperity, position, promotions, plaudits, or popularity. I don't have to be right, first, top, recognized, praised, regarded, or rewarded. I now live by presence, lean by faith, love by patience, lift by prayer, and labor by power.
>
> My face is set, my gait is fast, my goal is heaven, my road is narrow, my way is rough, my companions few, my Guide reliable, my mission clear. I cannot be bought, compromised,

detoured, lured away, turned back, diluted, or delayed. I will not flinch in the face of sacrifice, hesitate in the presence of adversity, negotiate at the table of the enemy, pander at the pool of popularity, or meander in the maze of mediocrity.

I won't give up, shut up, let up, burn up till I've preached up, prayed up, paid up, stored up, and stayed up for the cause of Christ. I am a disciple of Jesus. I must go till He comes, give till I drop, preach till all know, and work till He stops.

And when He comes to get His own, He'll have no problem recognizing me. His banner over me is clear.[3]

While I'm not sure who wrote those words, I believe Sameh certainly had them in his heart. It was evident by his life. I want them to be part of my life, but I am still a long way from there. In light of what Christ has done for me, I want to be part of the "Fellowship of the Unashamed" because honestly, the only thing that really matters is the gospel. Love trumped shame when Jesus bore the shame of the cross out of love. Love still trumps shame today. It is the power of God for the salvation of all who believe. Because of what God has done for us in Christ, let's live boldly—let's live openly—let's live out of our true identity as part of the fellowship of the unashamed.

13

To Live Out of Your True Identity, You Have to Die to the Old One

WHY A LIFE SUBMITTED TO CHRIST IS ACTUALLY THE LIFE YOU WANT

"How long will you waver between two opinions? If the LORD is God, follow him; but if Baal is God, follow him." But the people said nothing.

1 Kings 18:21

When Christ calls a man, he bids him come and die.

Dietrich Bonhoeffer

Suppose with me just for a moment that a wealthy man comes to you and asks you to build a house for him—the finest house money can buy. He's going to be traveling for two years, but when he comes back, he wants the house to be ready. He tells you that from time to time he will send an agent to check on your progress. He has full trust in you, but your integrity is on the line. You will be well paid, so you agree. He leaves, and your building work begins.

As the work unfolds, it dawns on you that you could actually buy cheaper materials for the house and pocket the cash. You start working the numbers in your head and realize you could make quite a bit more money that way. And he'd never know—how could he? Also, this is just a seasonal house for the man, so he's not going to be in it that much. So you skimp on the things that make the house a solid structure and instead spend a few dollars on dressing up the house so it looks good on the outside. The structure is weak, but the outside looks fabulous.

Along the way, construction materials are stolen by vandals. You replace those with cheaper products and keep going. Finally, you finish the house. It is a substandard, poorly built home, but from the outside it looks perfect. It is exactly as the man requested. You are the only one who knows the precarious nature of the structure and foundation.

Then one evening there is a knock at your door. A somewhat familiar-looking man stands in your doorway. It turns out to be the brother of the man who asked you to build the house. He tells you that his brother has been delayed from coming home because of other responsibilities, but because you have waited so long and worked so hard to make the house exactly as he desired, he is giving the house to you. It is his gift to you and your family. It is completely paid for, and any leftover money also belongs to you.

The brother hands you the deed and disappears into the night. You close the door and stare at the deed in disbelief. It suddenly and painfully dawns on you that you have picked your own pocket. The house you built will never stand, because you cheated on the foundation. How sad and disappointed you feel.[1]

Ravi Zacharias tells that story in his most recent book, *Has Christianity Failed You?* It may well be our story today. We are all building a house. We have all been given the resources and materials necessary to create a life that honors the Master. Living out of our true identity, authentically, as the sons and daughters of God is what I believe truly glorifies God. While living that way is rich in blessing, meaning, and purpose, I would be disingenuous if I did not also say that it is hard. As I have already said, it takes time and courage. We need to consider this reality as we think about how to move forward. We need to count the cost.

As we consider the necessary sacrifice of living faithfully—yielding our will to the will of the Father—I wonder if it is possible that we are holding back some of what we should commit to the project. We want to follow Christ part of the way, at least until it begins to cost too much. There is a cost/benefit analysis that we have done subconsciously in our minds. We don't want to follow so far that it becomes counterproductive to what we want.

We build, but are we holding back on the Master's project? If that's the case, do we actually wind up with the life (the house) we want, or is it somehow less? Have we, in effect, picked our own pockets? We're building, but our mind-set is not sold out to the Master. We're not all in on the project, yet we act surprised when our lives don't turn out to be as solid as we thought.

Are We Hungry for God?

This is the question that has plagued me for the past three years, and it is the root of my desire to write this book. For that reason, it is the topic of my concluding chapter.

I have been in ministry for twenty years. I have watched three different congregations in their approach to living as Christ's disciples. I have met with countless people and heard a myriad of problems and struggles. I have prayed and reflected and sought the Lord's counsel on what I have observed, not only in others but also in my own life. Through it all, I wonder why we seem to lack the authenticity of our faith. Why do we continue to be consumed by the world's standards for approval and worth? Why do we continue to care so much about what others think? At least part of the answer is that we're human. We're sinful. I get that.

However, I think at least part of the answer may be that we are picking our own pockets—and I'm not talking about money. I'm talking about our commitment to the gospel and the investment we make in being a disciple of Jesus Christ. Don't get me wrong, I think most who claim Christian faith genuinely love God, but honestly, I don't think most are *hungry* for God. There's nothing that is spiritually stirred in us. I don't think we actually grasp that true life is found *only* in Christ. We live in a gray twilight without spark or flame.

As a pastor, I bear responsibility for a particular Christian body. It's not for lack of effort, but somehow I have failed to teach and inspire the people I serve to devote their lives fully to the living God. I have confided in trusted friends who assured me, "David, you're part of a mainline denomination. Attendance all over the country is down. The fact that your church is stagnant is actually good news. At least you're not losing ground." Or they'll say, "David, younger generations and seekers are not going to come to a Presbyterian church, because they don't know what that is. That's just hard to overcome." I guess I don't find such words comforting.

I have studied the book of Acts, and what I find is that when the Word of God is proclaimed and his people respond in faithfulness, the church grows with a particular spiritual fire: hunger for a life of discipleship and service. I have often prayed for one of those Holy Spirit moments found in Acts when the Spirit blew through a place, creating exactly that kind of hunger and renewal. Here are just a few of the descriptions of what took place in the early church:

> Those who accepted his message were baptized, and about three thousand were added to their number that day. (Acts 2:41)

> And the Lord added to their number daily those who were being saved. (Acts 2:47)

> But many who heard the message believed; so the number of men who believed grew to about five thousand. (Acts 4:4)

> So the word of God spread. The number of disciples in Jerusalem increased rapidly. (Acts 6:7)

> Then the church throughout Judea, Galilee and Samaria enjoyed a time of peace and was strengthened. Living in the fear of the Lord and encouraged by the Holy Spirit, it increased in numbers. (Acts 9:31)

The Word of God spreads. The church grows and becomes hungry for more of God. The church and her people catch fire. Sure, we'll face opposition, but we are emboldened by the Holy Spirit, and just as the persecution of the early church fanned the flame of the gospel and grew the church, so it should today. Yet it does not. In this country, Christian faith is moving out, not in. Christian faith is losing influence, not gaining it.

Counting the Cost

In spite of the evidence, I'm not sure we believe that. Mostly, we are comfortable. We think our churches are doing just fine and our spiritual lives are right where they need to be. That may be true, but are we a little too satisfied? Have we learned all we want to about faith? Do we hunger merely for effective programs that meet our needs and make us happy, or do we hunger for God? Are we willing to sacrifice and suffer in order to build a life and a church that glorifies God? David Platt writes in *Radical*:

> We think Christianity's object is me. Me. Therefore, when I look for a church, I look for the music that best fits me and the programs that best cater to me and my family. When I make plans for my life and my career, it is about what works for me and my family. This is the version of Christianity that largely prevails in our culture.[2]

As such, people have no commitment to a body, no sense of investment in a community. They come and go on a whim based on what they need or what they want. If they don't like something that happens or a conflict arises, they just go somewhere else.

Contrast that with what Gerald Sittser writes about the early Christian martyrs in his book *Water from a Deep Well*:

> We will never truly understand Christianity unless we grasp the significance of martyrdom. The early Christians died because they confessed Jesus Christ as Lord. His lordship challenged all other ultimate claims on their lives—wealth, status, power and Rome itself. They believed Jesus tolerates no rivals. When forced to choose, they chose to follow Jesus, no matter what the price.[3]

It is doubtful that any of us will ever be required to make such a decision, but it does not change the fact that the lordship of Jesus Christ challenges all other claims on our lives. He is Lord, and he tolerates no rivals. I am tired of a satisfied, lethargic, culturally conditioned church that accepts a false gospel that does not stand on the singular truth that "there is no other name under heaven given to mankind by which we must be saved" (Acts 4:12). Christ allows no other god and no other rivals, and at some point in our lives, we must choose.

A Call to Choose

One of the great moments of choice in all of Scripture is found in 1 Kings 18. We are not the first community of God's people to struggle with such a choice. The people of Israel had been charged and called to build his temple—to be God's people—to be those through whom God would reveal himself to the world, and yet they wandered after other gods. In spite of all they had seen come from the hand of God, in spite of hearing his voice and seeing his work, they disobeyed his commands and sought the pagan gods of their culture.

The text tells us they worshiped Baal, which is actually a single word that represents multiple pagan gods. Therefore, the prophet Elijah took the initiative. He called the people of Israel together along with their leaders and said, "How long will you waver between two opinions? If the LORD is God, follow him; but if Baal is God, follow him." And what happened? "The people said nothing" (1 Kings 18:21). I believe that same question is directed at us.

God was essentially saying, "Look. You have to choose. You are living for yourself and following after false gods. Decide who is really God, and follow him." As challenging as that sounds, here's the stunning part: The people offered no response. They didn't say a word. Nothing. I would have hoped they would jump to their feet and exclaim, "Oh Lord, we have seen the work of your hand and the wonder of your love, and we know that you are the one true God! We know this life is nothing compared to the glory of the life that is to come. We will follow you alone!"

That's not what they did, is it? They couldn't decide, and so they were silent before the living God. I wonder if that may be who we are today. On her last show on May 25, 2011, Oprah Winfrey made it clear that she believes the one we need to follow is ourselves. The self. We are responsible for following the "energy"[4] of this world until it leads us to a place of happiness. She packages it beautifully, but it is a life and a dead end that entices many people. The result is that we waver between our core faith in Christ and the *feel-good* message of positive energy flowing from Oprah and many others today. How long will we waver between two opinions? How long will we be silent before God? Our silence may well define us, but if we understand the truth contained in Elijah's words, we will be silent no longer.

Urgency to Our Task

Elijah asks in 1 Kings 18:21, "How long?" Those are *time* words. Elijah is communicating that there is urgency to the task at hand. This is not child's play. There is kingdom work that needs to be done, and God is tired of waiting for Israel to decide whom they are going to follow. This tells us that God's patience is not unlimited and the message of the gospel is the most urgent need in our world today.

Several weeks ago I was at a dinner with Steve Douglass, the president of Campus Crusade for Christ. He travels all over the world, and I believe he has a distinct grasp of what is happening in global Christianity. He said that this time in world history is unique because for the past twenty-five years, people have had an increasing spiritual hunger. There has been a growing search for ultimate things. When combined with the chaos of crashing economies, international conflicts, and threats of terrorism, people are even more anxious and afraid, which adds fuel to the fire of their search.

Mr. Douglass went on to say, "In light of that, where is the most likely place these people will search? The church. And yet the church in America is not growing; it is shrinking. Somehow the church is failing to answer the questions that so many have during a time of perhaps her greatest opportunity." We may not realize it, but we may well be at the apex of human history—a time that will slip by us unless we seize it. Hungry, dying people yearn to know the light of life, yet they cannot find it because we have decided to follow a Christianity that focuses on us and not the building of God's kingdom.

We have slowly but most definitely jettisoned any trust in God's Word, instead believing our faith is what we make it. It has become a *me-centered* faith, not *Christ-centered*. I believe God is calling his church to step into our culture as salt and light, speaking boldly the gospel God has given us, rather than shrinking back from it because it may be hard or may require something of us. Like the martyrs of the early church, when forced to choose, let us choose Christ no matter the price.

Why We Waver

In counting the cost of making a choice to follow Jesus, we will remain unable to choose unless we address the issue of our wavering. Elijah asks, "How long will you *waver* between two opinions?" (1 Kings 18:21, emphasis added). *Waver*, in Hebrew, means someone is either lame or "walking without balance, listing from side to side." It is like watching a drunk person try to walk a straight line. Elijah is saying that we wobble from side to side, unable to choose to walk the straight line.

Does your life ever feel that way? Do you ever feel you are out of balance—that something is just not right? And is it possible that your sense of imbalance stems from your inability to choose whom you are going to follow? Jesus makes it quite clear in Matthew 6:24: "No one can serve two masters." We can't, but my goodness, we're sure trying.

We're not just serving two masters—it may as well be twenty-two. We can't commit to the Lord because there are so many things vying for our time and attention, so many things that lure us and promise us the life we seek, so many things that promise to give us the answers we need. I was stunned to read that in a recent survey of evangelical Christians, 60 percent said they believe there are multiple ways to salvation, not just Christ.[5] We have been lulled into a false gospel that compromises the unique work of the cross in favor of a cultural approach that is easier and less offensive.

Years ago Arthur Peacocke, on the faculty of theology at Oxford, wrote, "To be truly evangelical, the church of the next millennium will need a theology that will necessarily have to be genuinely liberal . . . to have any viability, it may well have to be stripped down to newly conceived essentials, minimalist in its affirmations."[6] How prophetic. Is that not what so many Christian churches have become? We are minimalists—minimalist in our approach to marriage and sexuality, minimalist in our approach to money, minimalist in our approach to the sacred nature of life, and minimalist in our approach to worship and the church.

We try to get along and look politically correct on the outside, but that will never change our culture, and it will never transform the human heart. We linger, doing as little as we can, and yet we feel confused as to why our lives feel as though they are careening from side to side, out of balance and off the line.

We waver, and we waver because of Baal. To worship Baal was to be fully engaged in worshiping the idols of the day, and that same practice is certainly in vogue today. Sittser said that Jesus will challenge "all other ultimate claims" on our lives, meaning Jesus will challenge every idol we have, every single thing we love more than we love God. That's what an idol is—a Jesus rival—and we have many:

- We make an idol of our appearance. Being physically, even sexually, attractive is the measure of our worth.
- We make an idol of our skin, our figure, our weight, and our muscles.
- We make an idol of sexual expression and desire, claiming that if we desire someone of our own gender or someone other than our spouse it must be okay, because otherwise God would never have allowed the desire. All the while we are forgetting that our desires are fallen and corrupt to begin with.
- We make an idol of our money. We clutch and hold it as though it belongs to us, as if fulfilling our material desires and competing with the belongings of others is the true measure of success.
- We make an idol of our reputation so that we are willing to compromise the gospel in order to ensure that others think of us in a particular light. Our focus becomes who we know and how we can manipulate those relationships for personal ends.
- We even make an idol of the church as if somehow following a denomination is the same thing as following Christ.
- We make an idol of our buildings as if somehow the size of our structure and the beauty of our walls is the

measure of who we are in Christ. Believers in Jesus, could we die to our buildings? If God called us to, could we walk away from these physical structures and worship in a warehouse because our hunger for God was so strong that we were willing to put our property on the altar?

What are your rivals to Jesus today? What are your idols?

The Call to Come and Die

Dietrich Bonhoeffer, the German theologian martyred in a Nazi prison camp, wrote, "When Christ calls a man, he bids him come and die."[7] Jesus says in Matthew 16:24, "Whoever wants to be my disciple must deny themselves and take up their cross and follow me." Jesus says in Revelation 3:15–16, "I know . . . that you are neither hot nor cold. I wish you were either one or the other! So, because you are lukewarm—neither cold nor hot—I am about to spit you out of my mouth." We are so much about self today, even in our walk with God. Churches are about their slogans, their programs, and doing all they can to be attractive to the culture. But they are not prepared to spiritually die, to sacrifice. Self-denial? No. Self-indulgence? Sure.

One church says, "Join us: We have open hearts and open minds." Another church slogan is "Passionate about Life." Another is "A Church Distributed." Here at First Presbyterian Church, ours is "Seek, Share, Serve." All are good slogans, but the invitation of Christ, the true slogan we should post on our walls, is this: "Come and Die." As David Platt asks, how do you think that would go over? Would it create a huge rush of new attendance? Hardly, and yet that is the message of the gospel. The church of Jesus Christ demands nothing less than our lives. We must die to the idols of our lives, die to a gospel of our own creation that allows us to live according to our own whims and never challenges our own desire, and die to ourselves in every way so only Jesus is lifted up.

As the Israelites considered what God through Elijah presented to them, they could not choose. They were frozen. The Israelites kept their mouths shut. So what did Elijah do? He set up a showdown. You probably know the story. He rallied 450 of the prophets of Baal and set up dueling sacrifices (1 Kings 18:16–40). Elijah gave the prophets the chance to call down their gods to consume the sacrifice, but over and over again they failed. Then Elijah called on God, and fire came down and consumed the wood.

Elijah gave them a contest. Sometimes I think we would prefer that. On more than one occasion, people have said to me, "It would be so much easier if God would appear to me. It would be easier if I could have a sure way of knowing." We want God to set up a duel, don't we? We want to put a test before God. "God," we say, "if you will come down and do this thing, then I'll believe. Then I will commit my life to you. If you will defeat this stronghold or power or issue in my life, then I'll follow you."

You want a contest? You waver and can't decide, so you want a little proof? Would a contest help you out? I've got a contest for you. How about Jesus versus death? How about taking a look at Jesus, who heard the command of the Father to come and die and obediently did so, suffering in agony and standing in the place of judgment and wrath where we belonged, hanging until he entered into death and hell, being fully separated from the Father's eternal love?

Satan danced on that grave that Saturday, danced in victory, danced that he had won. But the contest was not over. On the third day, God said, "Jesus, get up. Rise up. Death cannot contain you. Sin and evil cannot defeat you." Jesus rose up from the grave and bore witness to hundreds of people before ascending to the right hand of the Father.

There's your contest. Respond to it. It's time. By the power of the Holy Spirit, it is time for us to rise up with Christ. It is the time of our revival, because it is the time when we choose to die to self. Jesse Penn-Lewis, historian of the great Welsh revival of 1904, wrote:

> The hour of revival is a time of crisis and possible catastrophe. A crisis in the history of every individual, as well as in the history of a country, a church, or a district. A crisis for the unregenerate man, wherein he settles his eternal destiny, as he accepts or rejects conversion to God; a crisis to those who receive the fullness of the Holy Spirit, and to those who reject Him; for to the believer who bends and receives the Holy Spirit, it is the day of visitation of the Most High, but to others, it means the decision whether they will become spiritual men or remain carnal, whether they will elect to remain in defeat in their personal life, or determine to press on as overcomers.[8]

That is the crisis that has come to us. Will we overcome? Will we remain silent, or will we choose? God asks us, "How long will you waver? If I am truly God, then follow me—and if you decide I'm not, then go and follow your idols—but choose." This I know for sure: our choosing is also our dying. We will either die because we choose to live apart from God, or we will die to ourselves so that we can live for God. Each choice requires a death, but only one leads to life.

C. S. Lewis is one of my favorite authors, and I think he sums up the connection between our relationship with God and our ability to learn who we really are:

> Give up yourself and you will find your real self. Lose your life and you will save it. Submit to death, the death of your

ambitions and favorite wishes every day and the death of your whole body in the end: Submit with every fiber of your being, and you will find eternal life. Keep back nothing. Nothing that you have not given away will be really yours. Nothing in you that has not died will ever be raised from the dead. Look for yourself, and you will find in the long run only hatred, loneliness, despair, rage, ruin, and decay. But look for Christ and you will find Him, and with him everything else thrown in.[9]

This is the enormous challenge of *learning to be you*. I pray that you will consider the wonder of your true identity given to you by God. I pray that you will live out of that identity with bold confidence. I pray that as you go deeper in your relationship with God, he will illuminate more fully who you are. I pray that you will be patient and faithful as God does his sanctifying work in you. And I pray that you will die to the idols of our time—the idol of self—and commit fully to follow the Lord Jesus Christ. That's when you learn who you really are—when you give up yourself. That's the paradox of the Christian life. It is why the world so often does not understand. That's the authentic life God calls us to, but we only get there when we let go of the life we currently have. *Come and die.* Not a bad way to live.

Notes

Chapter 1 An Honest Struggle

1. "For the Record," *Sports Illustrated*, July 5, 2010, 12.

2. Ayn Rand, *Atlas Shrugged* (New York: Random House, 1957), appendix.

3. Thomas Kelly, *A Testament of Devotion* (New York: Harper and Brothers, 1941), 121.

4. Ravi Zacharias, *Has Christianity Failed You?* (Grand Rapids: Zondervan, 2010), 34.

Chapter 2 A God We Can Know

1. Bill Bright, *God: Discover His Character* (Orlando, FL: New Life Publications, 1999), 13.

2. Samuel Harris, *Letter to a Christian Nation* (New York: Knopf, 2006), ix.

3. Richard Dawkins, *The God Delusion* (New York: Bantam, 2006), 51.

4. Christopher Hitchens, *God Is Not Great: How Religion Poisons Everything* (New York: Twelve, 2007).

5. J. I. Packer, *Knowing God* (Downers Grove, IL: InterVarsity, 1973), 29.

6. Bright, *God: Discover His Character*, 15.

Chapter 3 Hide and Seek

1. Daniel Pink, *A Whole New Mind* (New York: Riverhead, 2005), 35.
2. "Mother Says Daughter's Class Picture Was Doctored," WFTV .com, October 12, 2006, http://www.wftv.com/news/news/mother-says -daughters-class-picture-was-doctored/nD9cj/.
3. John Powell, *Why Am I Afraid to Tell You Who I Am?* (Valencia, CA: Tabor, 1969), 12.
4. C. S. Lewis, *The Weight of Glory* (San Francisco: Harper Books, 1949), 26.
5. Brennan Manning, *Abba's Child* (Colorado Springs: NavPress, 1994), 31.
6. John Baillie, *A Diary of Private Prayer* (New York: Simon and Schuster, 1949), 53.

Part 2 Finding Our True Identity

1. Lisa Ling, "Pray the Gay Away?," *Our America with Lisa Ling*, Oprah Winfrey Network, March 8, 2011. See http://www.oprah.com /own-our-america-lisa-ling/Pray-the-Gay-Away-Can-you-be-gay-and -Christian.

Chapter 4 Why Do I Feel So Empty?

1. Tim Challies, "Facebook Makes Us Miserable," Challies.com, March 14, 2011, http://www.challies.com/christian-living/facebook-makes -us-miserable.
2. Lewis, *The Weight of Glory*, 41, emphasis added.
3. Karl Barth, *Church Dogmatics*, vol. 2, part 1 (Edinburgh: T&T Clark, 1957), 641.
4. Gerald Sittser, *Love One Another* (Downers Grove, IL: InterVarsity, 2008), 14.
5. Randy Frazee, *The Connecting Church* (Grand Rapids: Zondervan), 85.
6. Francis Schaeffer, quoted in Andy Stanley, *Christian Community* (Sisters, OR: Multnomah, 2004), 44.
7. Sittser, *Love One Another*, 19.

Chapter 5 Does My Life Make a Difference?

1. Bright, *God: Discover His Character*, 55.
2. C. S. Lewis, *Prince Caspian* (New York: Collier, 1951), 57.

Chapter 6 Why Am I Alone?

1. April Dembosky, "Tour of Embraces Makes a Stop in Manhattan," *New York Times*, July 10, 2008.

2. Bright, *God: Discover His Character*, 64.

3. Ibid., 73.

Chapter 7 Why Can't I Make Sense of My Life?

1. Bright, *God: Discover His Character*, 85.

2. Charles Spurgeon, *The Treasury of David Bible Commentary* (London: Funk and Wagnalls, 1886), 33.

3. Packer, *Knowing God*, 37.

Chapter 8 How Can I Get Rid of My Baggage?

1. *Webster's New Ideal Dictionary*, s.v. "freedom."

2. Hitchens, *God Is Not Great*, 9.

3. Michael Onfray, *In Defense of Atheism* (Toronto: Viking, 2007), 71.

4. Dawkins, *The God Delusion*, 22.

5. Tim Padgett, "Colombia's Stunning Hostage Rescue," *Time*, July 2, 2008.

Chapter 10 Why Do I Feel So Bad about Myself?

1. Bright, *God: Discover His Character*, 211.

2. Ibid., 212.

3. Ann Voskamp, "They Come Together," *A Holy Experience* (blog), October 27, 2008, www.AHolyExperience.com/2008/10.

4. Will Blythe, *To Hate Like This Is to Be Happy Forever* (San Francisco: Harper, 2009), 285.

Chapter 11 Why Is This Taking So Long?

1. Associated Press, "McDonald's the Holy Grail for Potato Farmers," MSNBC.com, September 2009, http://www.msnbc.msn.com/id/32983108/ns/business-us_business/t/mcdonalds-holy-grail-potato-farmers/.

2. Ibid.

3. John Stott, *The Message of 1 and 2 Thessalonians* (Downer's Grove, IL: InterVarsity, 1994), 76.

4. F. F. Bruce, ed., *The International Bible Commentary*, 1 Thessalonians 4 (Grand Rapids: Zondervan, 1999).

5. Dallas Willard, *Knowing Christ Today: Why We Can Trust Spiritual Knowledge* (New York: HarperOne, 2009), 92.

6. C. H. Spurgeon, "Prodigal Love for the Prodigal Son" (sermon, Metropolitan Tabernacle, London, March 29, 1891).

Chapter 12 Unashamed

1. *Webster's New Ideal Dictionary*, s.v. "shame."

2. Po Bronson, "How We Spend Our Leisure Time," *Time*, October 23, 2006.

3. Bob Moorehead, *Words Aptly Spoken* (Redmond, WA: Overlake Christian Bookstore, 1995).

Chapter 13 To Live Out of Your True Identity, You Have to Die to the Old One

1. Zacharias, *Has Christianity Failed You?*, 181.

2. David Platt, *Radical* (Colorado Springs: Multnomah, 2010), 70.

3. Gerald Sittser, *Water from a Deep Well* (Downers Grove, IL: InterVarsity, 2010), 28.

4. Oprah Winfrey, *The Oprah Winfrey Show*, ABC Television, May 25, 2011.

5. "Many Americans Say Other Faiths Can Lead to Eternal Life," *Pew Forum on Religion and Public Life*, December 18, 2008, http://www.pewforum.org/Many-Americans-Say-Other-Faiths-Can-Lead-to-Eternal-Life.aspx.

6. Arthur Peacocke, *The Palace of Glory: God's World and Science* (Washington, DC: AFT Press, 2005), 56.

7. Dietrich Bonhoeffer, *The Cost of Discipleship* (New York: Simon and Schuster, 1995), 89.

8. Jessie Penn-Lewis with Evan Roberts, *War on the Saints* (1912), chapter 12, unabridged edition available online at http://www.acts1711.com/wots.html.

9. C. S. Lewis, *Mere Christianity* (New York: Macmillan, 1958), 175.

David D. Swanson is senior pastor of the 5,000-member First Presbyterian Church of Orlando. He speaks at retreats, conferences, and churches throughout the United States and is engaged in a national media teaching ministry called The Well. He has been married to his wife, Leigh, for twenty-three years, and they have three teenage children. He lives in Florida.